nt. 1224-
2100
MITI

WINTER

SERVANE GIOL

# THE QUEEN OF THE DOLOMITES

# LIVING IN CORTINA D'AMPEZZO

PHOTOGRAPHS BY
MATTIA AQUILA

Marsilio Arte

AMORE
RIPARAZIONE

# CORTINA IN MY HEART

For me Cortina is Home. With a capital H.
As has ever been the case, and rightly so, the course of a child's life is determined by the choices of his or her parents, and this is also true for the places that, for better or worse, become part of the most profound essence of our being. My parents, in different ways and with different modes of expression, loved the place deeply and they have passed that love on to me in full. That is not always how things work out, but in my case, thank heavens, "my" Cortina has been and remains synonymous with wellbeing and beauty. Born at the end of September, I started to "frequent" it at the age of just over two months and since then it has always stayed close to my heart. The schools, the local friendships as well as the "seasonal" ones, which in a few rare and precious cases have lasted to the present day. Social life and the silence of the woods, the succession of the seasons, including those of life. Getting stuck in traffic on the way there and then all of a sudden the wonder of a stroll in the semi-deserted center or the spectacle of the moon, the mountains, and the valley from somewhere a little higher up. The continual practice of sport, as a training ground of daring and then as lifestyle. The amazing energy my mother displayed in entertaining her more or less true friends, the breakfasts that would last all the way up to the beginning of amazing lunches, the house always filled with people of every kind and then wonderfully deserted for months on end. Via Marangoi, home for me in the true sense of the word, which for fifty years has signified a refuge, the inner side of "my" Cortina.
An alternation of normality and mundanity, family intimacy, and extreme sociality at every hour of the day. The "flavor" is still there, pieces of furniture and objects that one might not have expected, mixed up in a vision of taste in the interiors that make that fine chalet of Gigi Vietti's, another unforgettable friend, "Marta's house" forever. I've met, and it seemed quite normal, stars from every field (culture, sport, politics, business, entertainment); along with wackos, low lifes and scroungers of every kind who rendered the peace and quiet that reigned off season even more precious. Marvelously imperfect: by nature I prefer it discreet and not crowded as in the past, but I try to keep up the tradition, remaining open at least to sparkling New Year's Eve parties and the occasional pleasant get-together with old and new friends.

MATTEO MARZOTTO

# CORTINA'S DUALITY

Cortina d'Ampezzo—the name sets the tone. Above all, don't make the mistake of forgetting the second part.

Historically divided between the Austrian Tyrol (for four hundred years) and the Italian Veneto, Cortina d'Ampezzo has consciously or unconsciously cultivated the duality of its culture.

It has two nicknames as well: for some it is the "Queen of the Dolomites" and for others the "Pearl," perhaps due to its incredible geographical location, a small white town at the center of a valley surrounded by jagged mountains that can call to mind the shell of an oyster.

Its language is dual too, Ladino and Italian are both used by the people of Ampezzo.

But it is above all the duality of its seasons that attracts tourists: summer and winter, with spring and fall deliberately forgotten.

Its biggest challenge, like any seasonal resort, is to reconcile two often opposing interests, that of its residents and that of its ever-growing number of visitors.

The Olympic Games of 1956 were the spark for an infatuation with the place that continues unabated, and after seventy years the torch will be returning here in 2026. Those first games turned an upscale village frequented by royalty and a few daring English climbers in the nineteenth century into a winter sports resort, and then the movies made it a place where the whole of Italy wanted to go for their vacations.

This multicolored dualism is reflected in the valley's houses, not only on the outside, built half of stone and half of wood, but also on the inside: by keeping the traditional elements of Tyrol, such as the *stuben* and *stufe*, the Veneto is not to be outdone with its stucco, filigree, and glass. The people of Cortina not only learned how to work with materials like wood and silver, but went on to become past masters of the techniques. The filigree of Cortina has no equal, even though the secret of its fineness has been lost over time. Wood has its Tarkashi and its sculptors, including the great Andrea Brustolon, and those masterpieces of the past the *stube* are still dismantled when houses are sold and reassembled elsewhere.

In the winter this tradition of excellence is translated into sporting prowess. Some great champions have been born in the valley, in all the disciplines, from bobsleigh to ice hockey and the more media prominent skiing. Adrenaline is the common driving force in climbing and speed sports, in both summer and winter. Challenge, commitment, the love of nature. But the prime mover in Cortina d'Ampezzo can be found in a notion that seems rather outdated these days: courage. Human courage in the face of nature. The courage of men pitted against men like those soldiers of the First World War whose traces can be found all over the mountains; the courage of the early climbers, of the mountain rescue teams, of the first skiers, of the first people to make a ski jump. The courage to be the first. The courage of excellence.

Ernest Hemingway said of Cortina d'Ampezzo that it "is in the swellest country on earth. [...] It is the loveliest country I've ever known." Perhaps he was talking about the art of living, the appeal of a certain wholly Italian *dolce vita*, made up of *enrosadira* admired from Pecol, of aperitifs at the Hotel de la Poste and such culinary delights as the stuffed pasta called *cazunzei* or raspberry pie. For athletes though, Cortina is anything but gentle, with the steepness of its ski slopes, the jagged majesty of its dolomite rocks, rigorous in the summer and above all eternal, in the hope that its snows will be as well.

SERVANE GIOL

ZANGRANDI
GIRARDI
MICHIELLI
COSTANTINI
de ZANNA
ALVERA
de BEGONTINA
FRANCESCHI
COLLI-COLLE

# CONTENTS

CORTINA

CORTINA CORTINA CORTINA CORTINA CORTINA CORTINA CORTINA CORTINA CORTINA CORTINA CORTINA

# WINTER

CORTINA
CORTINA
CORTINA
CORTINA
CORTINA
CORTINA
CORTINA
CORTINA

# THE BIRTH OF WINTER SPORTS

*left*
A closet made out of old beams and vintage skis in Anna Marzotto's home

*below*
Skiers of yesteryear downhill racing in a photo from the 1920s/'30s. Zeno archive

## THE FIRST PAIR OF SKIS IN CORTINA

The very first pair of skis arrived in Cortina in 1897, brought there by Agostino Kolic, a Czech teacher at the Art School. The ski in question was two meters long, bent upward at the tip, with wicker bindings.
This "invention" of Norwegian origin was immediately copied and reproduced in people's homes, before certain families like the Valle or the Morotto began to specialize in making them.
At the time there were no ski slopes, the activity was immensely difficult and the clothing far from technical. A certain Federico Terschak was the main promoter of the new sport and set up cross-country, downhill and jumping competitions, as the three disciplines were still linked.
In 1903, the Sci Club Cortina was born, with a membership of forty. It is the oldest Italian club that is still active. In 1932, the FISI (Federazione Italiana Sport Invernali) organized the first courses aimed at standardizing instruction and training teachers of the new winter sport. Twenty-one teachers from Cortina earned their badge and on December 15, 1933, founded the first ski school in Italy authorized by the FISI.

The ski school offered courses at three levels of difficulty, for beginners, zip-line operators and competitive skiers. Beginners were confined to the so-called *campi*, or "nurseries" as they are known in English, i.e. to marked-off, enclosed areas. These amateurs were also regular spectators at sports events and users of the Cortina-Pocol chairlift.
More expert were the specialists in cross-country skiing. They left on foot from the center of Cortina and headed for Mount Faloria, with the Falzarego and Giau passes among the favorite routes.
The last group were the *sciatori da gara*, or competitive skiers. Native to the valley, they were the protagonists of all the challenges, launching themselves from the ramp at a height of twenty meters, or pitting themselves against one another in the earliest races.

The first competitions were held at Nuvolau and Cinque Torri in 1911, and the first international competition at Rumerlo, Campo Corona, in 1913. Cortina became the favorite destination of many of the new sport's enthusiasts and its reputation was carried beyond the national borders by the excellence of its practitioners.
Cortina soon began to produce champion skiers, including the Valle and Colli brothers and Ofelia Zardini, twice the female skiing champion of Italy.
Unusually for any kind of board sport, skiing has attracted many women since its creation.
The boom of the 1920s would be followed by a rapid development of mechanisms for transporting skiers uphill: the runs became more easily accessible, by means that ranged from the old but popular horse-drawn sled carrying skiers up to the alpine meadows of the Cinque Torri to the first cableway, built in 1925 and connecting Pocol with the center of Cortina, just beneath the Hotel de la Poste.
This cableway marked the beginning of a new era. It was the first in Italy to be used for the transport of the general public and skiers.
As levels of skill increased, the slopes of Pocol became too easy for some skiers, and so the Rumerlo sledge lift on the Tofane was built in 1936: a large sled carrying fifteen people hauled by a steel cable. It was so steep that people were advised not to turn around and look behind them.
In 1939 the Principe di Piemonte cableway on Monte Faloria proved to be a huge technological challenge for the time, with its ascent of nine hundred meters.

"THE TOFANA WAS ONE OF MY PASSIONS.
I WAS SO FAMILIAR WITH ITS PROFILE I COULD HAVE DRAWN IT WITH MY EYES CLOSED"

Milena Milani, *A Girl Called Jules*, 1966

*left*
A detail of the dining room
in Casa Gris Dainese

*top*
An elegant skier on the slopes
of Cortina, 1930s.
Giovanna and Filippo Cordova archive

*bottom*
A daring ascent on foot
in the 1920s/'30s. Zeno archive

> "THERE IS NOTHING LIKE SKIING AT CORTINA ON THE FRESHLY GROOMED TOFANA EARLY IN THE MORNING, ALONE. SILENCE ALL AROUND, FOOTSTEPS IN THE SNOW, NATURE AWAITING THE ARRIVAL OF THE FIRST SKIERS"

Marina Cicogna, *Ancora spero*, 2023

In the Zeno archive there is a rare photo of a female skier dated "Cortina 1924" that seems to have been the inspiration for a famous poster of the ENIT (Ente Nazionale Italiano del Turismo) from the 1920s

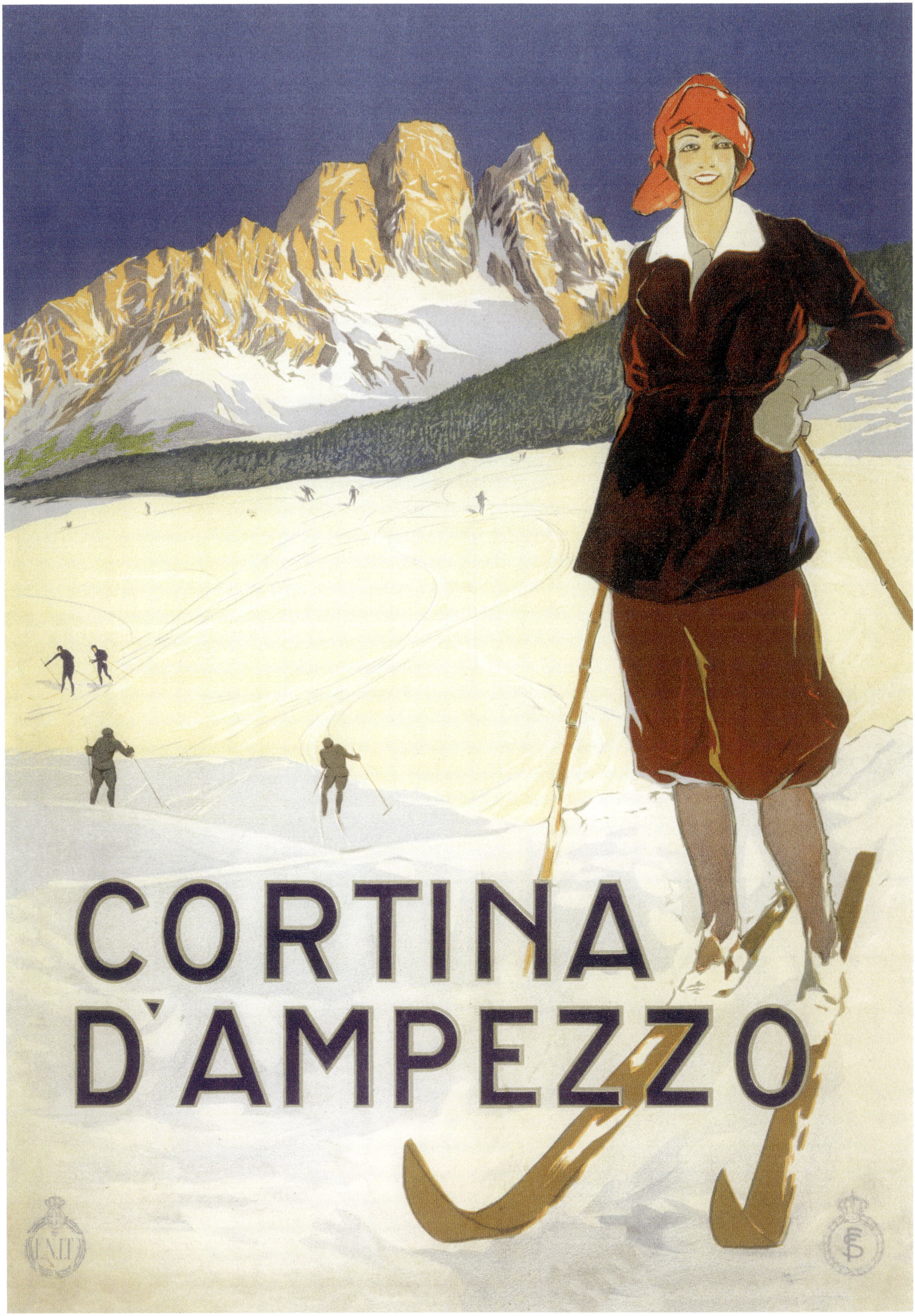
CORTINA
D'AMPEZZO

## THE BARON FRANCHETTI

All these innovations were made possible by the determination of one man: Baron Carlo Franchetti.
Carlo Franchetti (1896–1955), nicknamed *il barone Ruggente* or "the Roaring Baron," was the pioneer of modern skiing. Climber, spelunker, and ice cave expert, on which he would write a manual, he spent the Great War in the Dolomites as a training officer for the Alpini infantry and was awarded several medals. Madly in love with these mountains, he obtained the concession of mounts Tofane, Cristallo and Faloria for a hundred years.
He started by organizing rides for tourists in tracked Citroën vehicles, and then funded the first ski lifts through his company FAIT (Funivie Aeree Italiane Turistiche), whose name was a nod to FIAT... His success culminated in the technical feat of the Faloria cableway, which brought Cortina into the modern era. It was inaugurated on February 5, 1939, by Edda Ciano with a ceremony that included an intimate lunch.
Edda Ciano (1910–1995) was the rebellious daughter of Mussolini, as well as an opinion leader and great sportswoman. She would help focus the attention of the press and the public on Cortina as a resort and played a part in turning the emerging sport into a media attraction. According to her faithful guide Roberto Zardini, she was an indefatigable and courageous skier.
For six years, from 1935 until her last visit in 1941, the story of nights playing cards, drinking cocktails, and attending balls and other entertainments filled the gossip columns. She took up residence every Christmas at the Hotel Bellavista and devoted her days entirely to skiing. Every morning she would set off to hurtle down the snowclad slopes with the same group of loyal male friends. Besides the devoted Zardini, the group included Tito Lebreton, an antique dealer of Venetian origin who was Cortina's first interior designer, Counts Baldi and Nuvoletti and Baron Franchetti.
The latter named after her a refuge on Monte Faloria, whose inauguration was followed by a memorable schuss down to Cortina.
It is indicative of their excellent skiing skills that one of the faithful members of Edda's group became president of Sci Club 18 (Carlo Franchetti, from 1947–1955).

*left*
Small ceramic figurines representing people skiing or practicing other winter sports can be found in many homes in Cortina. Probably made locally in the 1940s/'50s, this one is in La Montanella

*top*
The first skiers between the wars reached the peaks aboard the Citroën tracked vehicles made available by Baron Franchetti. Here a photo from the 1920s/'30s. Zeno archive

*bottom*
Tito Lebreton in Cortina and with Edda Ciano in the 1930s in two rare photos from the De Girolami archive

## THE SCI CLUB 18

The Sci Club 18 was founded in 1930 at a bar in Rome by eighteen university friends united by a desire for political freedom and a passion for skiing. This marked the birth of a movement that would excite an entire intellectual and then entrepreneurial world made up of people like the brothers Nicolò and Luigi Donà dalle Rose, founders of Porto Rotondo in Sardinia, the legendary explorer Gianni Albertini, Fosco Maraini and Eugenio Monti.

As president, Carlo Franchetti worked toward the integration of the ski club, so that the originally Rome-based association gradually came to center on Cortina. Its membership was opened to women in the 1980s; Sci Club 18 is the only one to have its own club house and continues to train young champions, who proudly wear the red wool sweater with its distinctive crest.

*bottom*
The historical photo in the clubhouse of the Sci Club 18 is of the SC18-GUF meet in Milan in 1936

*right and following pages*
Interiors of the clubhouse with the historical logo, the many trophies won by members, and the dining room

FISI
FEDERAZIONE
ITALIANA
SPORT
INVERNALI
Cortina
COPPA ITALIA
MASTER
CORTINA 6-7 FEBBRAIO 2016
1 SOCIETA' CLASSIFICATA

18

“THE CANALONE IS LIKE ONE OF THOSE PEOPLE WHO HAVE A VERY REASONABLE CHARACTER BUT A MENACING COUNTENANCE”

Dino Buzzati, “È aumentata di statura.
Cortina stazione invernale,” in *Corriere d’informazione*, 1957

*left*
In Domitilla Clavarino’s home, a photograph by Slim Aarons from the famous series taken in Cortina in the 1960s

*top*
A group of young skiers toward the end of the 1950s. The second from the left is Lorian Franchetti; the second from the right is Simba Franchetti; the last on the right is Luigino Revedin. Franchetti archive

*right*
Nicolò Donà dalle Rose, great sportsman and member of the Sci Club 18, gets ready at the start of a competition at the end of the 1950s. Donà dalle Rose archive

*following pages*
In the lounge of Casa Modulo three panels from Fornasetti’s series *Lux Gstaadt*

IL TEMPO DEL RUGBY

AND ITS SPIRIT
LIFE IN A FRENCH COUNTRY HOUSE
ANDREA ODICINI
Rizzoli
Bruno Bellocchi
Rizzoli

SKIERS OF TODAY

Hubertus von Hohenlohe and his wife Simona Gandolfi are both winter sports enthusiasts. Simona, a talented skier, is first cousin of the champion Alberto Tomba. As for Hubertus, he holds the record for participation in the Winter Olympics, competing in a total of six men's downhill races. A jack of all trades, Hubertus is also an artist, photographer, and singer. He has designed the fabrics used in his home.

*previous pages*
Walls painted in a folk style go well with Slim Aarons's photographs in Casa Clavarino

MEX

VII GIOCHI OLIMPICI D'INVERNO
CORTINA D'AMPEZZO 1956

The logo of the 1956 Winter Olympic Games and two stages of the opening ceremony—bottom the lighting of the tripod—depicted on vintage postcards

## THE 1956 OLYMPIC GAMES: A TURNING POINT FOR CORTINA



An enthusiastic sportsman, figure skater, and member of the Olympic Committee, Count Alberto Bonacossa (1883–1953) worked for over ten years to bring the games to Cortina d'Ampezzo. He persuaded the town council to apply to hold the 1944 games, and this was accepted in 1939, but the event was canceled due to the outbreak of war. Its next application, for the 1952 Winter Games, was rejected in favor of Oslo in Norway.

On April 27, 1949, Cortina's third candidacy was successful, beating Lake Springs and Montreal. Unfortunately, Bonacossa would not see the games, as he died on January 30, 1953, three years before they were held.

The valley embarked on a race against time. Postwar developments had left Cortina impoverished and in poor shape. It was necessary to repair the town's infrastructure, including its roads and railroad lines, and even the telephone and electricity networks had to be extended since for the first time the games were going to be televized.

Thus the Posts and Telecommunications Office (1953–1955) and the building of the TELVE telephone company (1953–1954) were built in record time to a design by the architect Edoardo Gellner.

And the hotels, which had been turned into convalescence centers for the war-wounded, had to return to their original role.

"THE 1956 OLYMPIC GAMES FINALLY SET THE SEAL ON ITS VOCATION AS A TOURIST RESORT OF INTERNATIONAL SCOPE AND FAME"

Maria Cristina Todeschini, in *Cortina. Ritratto inedito di una signora*, 2002

The Olympic committee realized that the sports facilities did not meet their standards: there was no speed skating rink and the bobsleigh track and ski jump ramp were in poor condition. The ski slopes also needed to be brought up to date. Those of Col Druscié and the Tofana were upgraded, the first ski lifts were constructed, and a gondola cableway and chair lift were installed on Monte Faloria.

The Italian government contributed 460 million lire to funding the works, but the rest had to be raised from private sources. So the first sponsors were brought in: Fiat provided cars, while Olivetti supplied typewriters for the four hundred journalists covering the games.

Two now legendary places would see the light: the spectacular ski jump (with a HS or hill size of 100 meters) and the Ice Stadium. Both were built in typical 1950's style.

The seventh Winter Olympic Games were held from January 26 to February 5, 1956, with thirty-two countries taking part. For the first time the opening ceremony saw a woman, the skier Giuliana Chenal-Minuzzo, read out the Olympic oath. The Olympic flame, lit and blessed by the Pope in Rome, was carried by gifted athletes like Lino Lacedelli and Zeno Colò and the ascent to the Olympic cauldron was made on skates by Guido Caroli. The public was present, with over 14,000 seats for spectators, as was the President of the Republic at the time, Giovanni Gronchi, who declared the games open.

A total of 821 athletes took part, 689 men and 132 women, all of whom were housed in local hotels, while the facilities for competition were concentrated in the Ampezzo Valley. A rare, indeed unique aspect, all the sites were a very short distance apart.

The 1956 games were dominated by the Soviets. At the height of the Cold War, Nikita Khrushchev was determined to demonstrate the superiority of Communism and their participation raised the level of competition. In the twenty-eight events, the Soviets won seven gold medals, including the hotly contested ice hockey final against the USA. They also won three golds, a silver, and a bronze in speed skating.

The true hero of the Games was a young Austrian with the looks of a Hollywood film star from neighboring Austria (Kitzbühel). For the first time in the history of the games, Toni Sailer (1935–2009) would win all three gold medals in the three alpine skiing events: slalom, giant slalom, and downhill. It was a feat that has only been repeated once since then, by Jean-Claude Killy twelve years later. In the giant slalom the gap to second place was 6.2 seconds, the largest ever achieved up until then. It is interesting to note that the man who came second in the slalom was Chiharu Igaya from Japan, whose silver was the first ever medal won by Japan at the Winter Olympics.

The man who won most medals at the games was the Swedish cross-country skier Sixten Jernberg, with four.

Skiing in general was dominated by Austria, with the country's men and women taking nine of the eighteen medals.

The people of Cortina were proud to find that their bobsleigh track had produced real champions: Giacomo Luigi Conti (1918–1992) and Lamberto Dalla Costa (1920–1982) won gold in the two-man bobsleigh, with Eugenio Monti (1928–2003) and Renzo Alverà (1933–2005) taking silver.

Above all, the games would permanently change the town's mindset and geography. It became easy to access, while a new clientele in the

THE OLIMPIC SKI JUMP

The Olympic ski jump at Zuell di Sotto has undergone various modifications over time, bringing it to its current height of 100 m. In the images on these pages, taken from vintage postcards, the ski jump at the end of the 1950s and two amusing shots of athletes jumping. The two photos show the techniques utilized in the competition. Right, with arms raised in the traditional Norwegian technique; left, with the arms alongside the body, the innovative technique introduced by the Finnish skiers who eventually won gold and silver.

midst of an economic boom spurned the hotels and went hunting for sites on which to build their second homes despite the hotels. The majority of the chalets that can be seen today date from this period. As for the marks left by the Olympics on the valley, there are a multitude of them, ranging from the old ski ramp to the Ice Stadium. It is perhaps on its slopes that we can best understand the impetus given to the area by the Olympics: the Olimpia and Canalone pistes on the Tofana where the downhill and slalom races were held and the Vitelli on Mount Faloria where the men's giant slalom took place.
The great sportsmen of the 1950s, like Giovanni Dibona (1944) and Ilio Colli (1931–1953), continued to bring luster to the valley, as has the very popular Kristian Ghedina (1969) more recently.
Cortina d'Ampezzo will host the Winter Olympic Games again in 2026. This time the 25th games will be held over a much larger area, spread across Trentino-Alto Adige, Lombardy, and the Veneto.

*top*
A game of ice hockey was held every year at Christmas. In this fine image from the 1950s we can see: second from left, Dante Bini; third from left, Nicolò Donà dalle Rose; sixth from left, Piero Lucchini. In the middle of the front row, Anna Bozza, mascot of the Sci Club 18, excellent skier and great beauty of the day. Crouching, first from the right, a young Eugenio Monti. Donà dalle Rose archive

*above, left*
Young skaters in Cortina, late 1950s. Donà dalle Rose archive

*right and facing page*
The legendary changing rooms and wooden stands of the Ice Stadium in Cortina built for the 1956 Olympic Games and designed by the engineer Mario Ghedina and the architects Francesco Uras and Riccardo Nelli

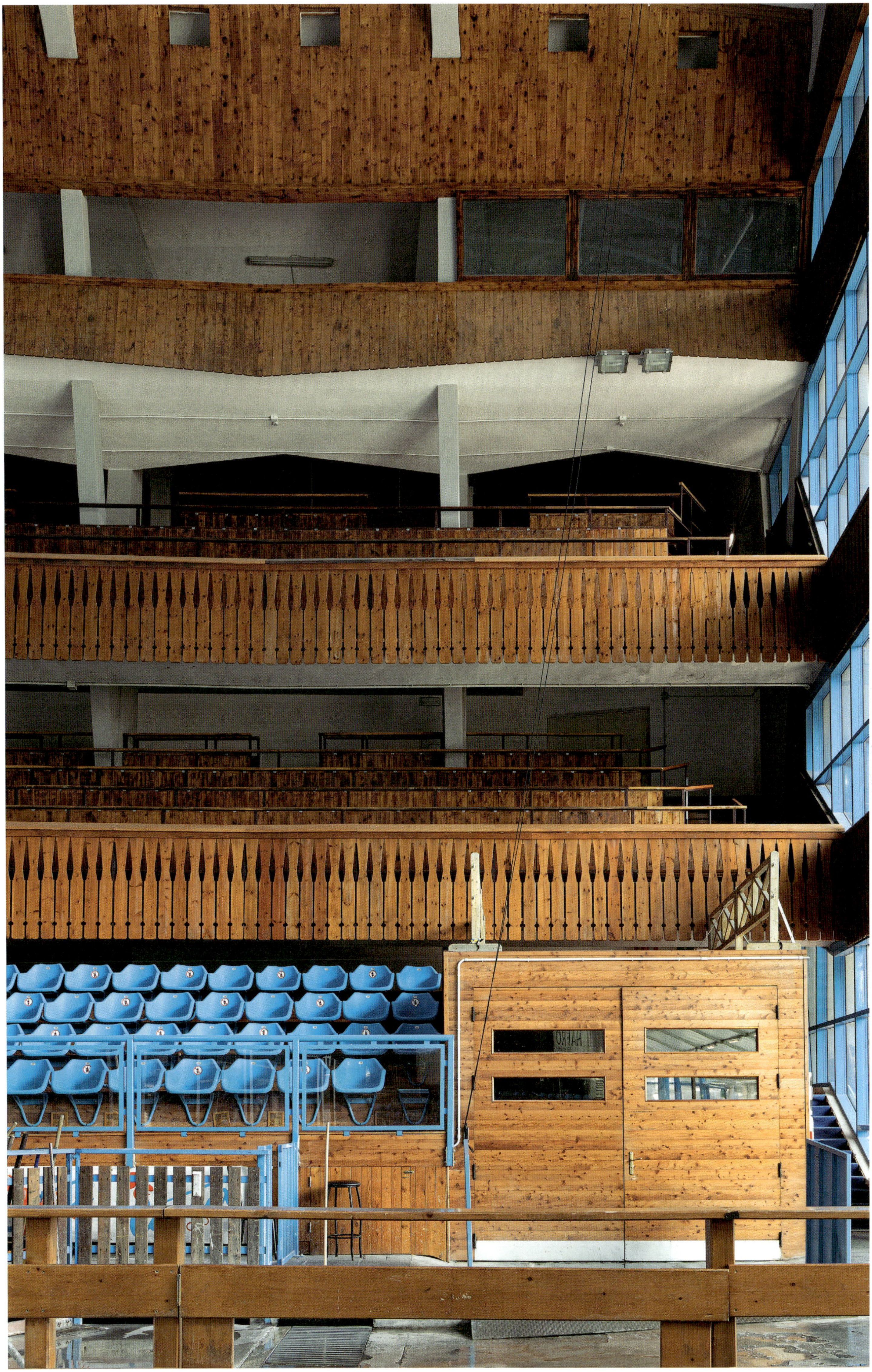

## SLED AND BOBSLEIGH

An indispensable accessory of every *losa* (the Ladin name for the large entrance hall of mountains houses), the sled is for use by any member of the family. Originally employed as a means of transport on snow, it has gradually turned into an object used for fun by every child and grown-up in the valley.

Outings by sled were initially organized by local families, but the custom was soon also taken up by tourists. So all the big hotels equipped themselves with dozens of sleds for their guests. The most popular descent was the one from Pocol to Lacedel. Over time they were modified to make them more comfortable: the wooden runners of the early sleds were covered with fabric to cushion the roughness of the terrain. Clothing, however, remained the same as in town: long skirts, leather ankle boots with laces...

Later, the quest for speed, and the thrill it produces, would change the sled's structure: it was fitted with a steering mechanism and brakes to create the *bobis* (from the English bobsleigh), a two-seater that was the extremely dangerous ancestor of the two-man bob and then of the five-man bob, invented in Switzerland.

Cortina was the first and for a long time the only place in Italy to have its own bobsleigh track. Inaugurated in 1923 at Ronco, it was 1,200 meters long. The local people are aficionados of this sport, and Cortina has produced several champions, including the brothers Antonio, Guido, and Uberto Gillarduzzi and Eugenio Monti.

For the 1956 Olympic Games the track was modernized and its length increased to 1,500 meters. It was also equipped with a stopwatch, a scoreboard, and stands.

*top and facing page*
Statuettes made out of various materials representing athletes in winter dress; above at Ca' Alleluia and right in another Cortina home

*left*
A group of excursionists on a sled in Cortina in 1924. Zeno archive

*left, top and right*
The Bob Club Cortina and the track
with the famous Cristallo curve
and wooden stands

*left, bottom*
In the home of a collector, a painting
of the historic run by Eugenio Monti's
four-man bob, winner of the silver medal
at the 1956 Winter Olympics

# SEEKING WARMTH

## FIREPLACES.
## VIETTI AND GELLNER: THE ARCHITECTS OF CORTINA

*left*
Marta Marzotto's home, Luigi Vietti designed a lounge with his hallmark raised hearth. Above the fireplace a collection of still lifes depicting various kinds of mushrooms

*following pages*
In a home in Cortina, a magnificent example of Luigi Vietti's style; a large fireplace built of hammered stone and wood; the traditional, slightly raised hearth in which sections of logs are embedded; and the classic couch upholstered in white plush

With the exception of a few chalets designed by the decorators Tito Lebreton in the 1940s and Renzo Mongiardino shortly afterward, the finest homes in Cortina bear just two names, those of Luigi Vietti and Edoardo Gellner. Luigi Vietti (1903–1998) was an Italian architect and urban planner dubbed "the inventor of the Cortina style." Graduating from Rome Sapienza University in 1928, he began to specialize in a new genre after the end of the war, the "vacation home," designing prestigious residences in locations that were beginning to turn into tourist resorts. Cortina d'Ampezzo become one of his "places of the soul."
He had discovered it in the 1930s, when it was just a small village with a few buildings inhabited by locals and surrounded by woods and meadows. He bought a tumbledown old *tabià*, a seventeenth-century wooden barn, and saved it by anchoring it to the rock.
When asked what characteristics a house in Cortina ought to have, he answered: "In Cortina, which is always pleasant and open, I would follow the example of the traditional Tyrolean houses, built half of plastered brick and half of wood." His house was based on an alternation of light and shade that reminded him of the play of sunlight and shadows in a forest, realized with great simplicity. "For some of the details I took my inspiration from the traditional costumes and furnishings of this region, such as the brightly-colored velvets that are matched in a distinctive way and the impression you get when entering the small mountain churches filled with flowers, greenery, and gilded objects." He faced the

"THE FIREPLACES ARE DECORATIVE AS WELL AS FUNCTIONAL, A FIREPLACE IN THE SUN AT HOME. I LOVE THEM DEEPLY, SO I ALWAYS TRY TO PUT ONE IN MY HOUSES"

Luigi Vietti, in *I camini di Vietti*, 1990

LUXURY HOTELS

bathrooms in his house with logs, and kept the sloping floors of the old chalets. Montanelli admired "his ability to design homes of great taste that retained a rustic air," (Indro Montanelli, "Siamo tutti pappagalli," in *Il Borghese*, 1955) and the architect himself admitted that "my true invention was to not invent anything but to follow with great attention and care this people's ancient knowledge of construction and understanding of how to live."

He specialized in homes for an upper middle-class and aristocratic Italian clientele, whose main requirement was to have a place where they could entertain without losing sight of the holiday spirit, all in harmony with the surrounding nature.

Out of this came some magnificent villas, first of all Villa Bella and La Montanella (1947–1948) for Indro Montanelli.

Vietti's style was always centered around the hearth. "The fireplace brings the sun into the home. I love it and always try to put one in my homes" (Luigi Vietti, in *I camini di Vietti*, 1990). He would design them for every taste and in every style: from fireplaces set in niches to ones raised on a platform in which sections of logs were sunk to create an intimate corner; and in all sorts of materials, river pebbles, brickwork, wood, stone... Certain elements are highly characteristic of Vietti's style, such as couches upholstered in white plush, the alternation of masonry and wood, a broad roof, and the reutilization of old-fashioned ceilings.

The fundamental principle of his Town plan of 1955–1956 was a renunciation of architectural novelty. He divided the valley in two: the Pocol side with the old hamlets that were the original nuclei of the town, which became an area where building was completely banned; and the opposite side in the direction of Faloria and Tre Croci, where most of the new constructions would go.

Another architect had worked on a Town plan in 1951, but it had been rejected. Edoardo Gellner (1909–2004) was an Italian architect of Austrian origin—born in the Italian Abbazia, now Opatija in Croazia—who designed the TELVE Building and the Post Office for the 1956 Olympic Games. He had discovered Cortina at the end of the 1930's and was so fascinated by the place that he moved his home and his architecture studio there in 1947. He modernized the complexes of the most prestigious hotels of the time, from the Cristallo to the Gran Albergo Bellavista, and formed a close friendship with Leo Menardi, who asked him to design a new type of chalet to serve as his home.

Thus Villa Menardi was born. It featured an explicit personal reworking of Frank Lloyd Wright's architecture in the use of natural materials such as stone and wood in the tavern on the ground floor. The same thing happened at the Hotel Miramonti with the hexagonal module in the false ceiling and the form of the tables, chairs and couches, making it closely resemble the bar of Lloyd Wright's Imperial Hotel in Tokyo.

Luigi Vietti's eclecticism can also be seen in the contrast between these two fireplaces he designed: a monumental stone one in Paola Caovilla's home, made in all likelihood out of elements salvaged from an old house, and a smaller, saffron-colored ceramic one for La Montanella

*left*
In a former barn skillfully converted by Luigi Vietti, the focal point of the living room is the curiously shaped fireplace embellished with a fine seventeenth-century Austrian chimneypiece and flanked by two wooden sculptures, also of Austrian provenance

*top*
A collection of silver matchboxes and lighters from various periods and origins

It is interesting to see how in Gellner's style "the individual pieces of furniture cannot be separated from the spatial conception of the whole. They, too, are architecture" (Franco Mancuso, *Edoardo Gellner*, 1996). The 1950s saw him engaged in drawing up a town plan that was of great importance in view of the Olympic Games to be held in 1956. Broadly speaking, the 1951 plan was based on the idea of a town organized into nuclei rather than as an expansion of the center. He also worked on the detailed plan for the center of Cortina in 1952 and designed seven buildings that were all constructed in the space of a few years (AGIP Motel, Residence Palace, Casa Giavi, Ca' del Cembro, and the children's hotel La Meridiana on top of the ones already mentioned).
The strong conflicts that arose from the construction of the TELVE Building led Gellner to make the momentous decision never to work in Cortina again. He wrote in his diary, "I have had to give in."
The architecture of Cortina d'Ampezzo, and its typically 1950's slightly retro appearance, owe a great deal to these two great figures.

*top*
Edoardo Gellner's most famous fireplace is located in the *stube* of the home he designed for the Menardi family, owners at the time of the nearby Hotel Cristallo. The house now belongs to Silvia Iliceto

*right*
The fireplace designed by Studio Gris Dainese for Casa Santel: a two-story monolith of black steel in a converted barn

## *STUBE* AND *STUFE*

In the traditional houses of Ampezzo only two rooms were heated, the kitchen and the *stube*, or *stüa* in Ladino. The latter was the room containing the *stufa*, a wood-burning ceramic stove.
The very name *stube* is indissolubly linked to the quest for warmth. While the etymology of the word is uncertain, it may derive from the Latin *extufare*, to heat, origin of the French term for a stove, *étuve*. This heated room has been present in all the villages of the Alps and the adjacent valleys since the thirteenth century. It originated in the homes of the nobility, and from there spread to the homes of the clergy and then the peasantry.
This room could be considered, like the kitchen, the heart of the house. It was the hub of family and social life. The *stube* was also a reflection of the social status of its owner. It contained photos of the family, along with the most precious objects.
To earn the name of a *stube* it had to adhere to precise rules: a regular plan of great simplicity, with the stove in one corner, and in the opposite corner a table around which ran a bench set in the walls. This room was always located on the sunny side of the house, with from two to four windows to let in light.
Above the table was the Lord's corner (*Herrgottswinkel*), where a crucifix hung, surrounded by religious images. A vase of flowers and an ivy plant completed the decoration of the *Herrgottswinkel*. It is where grace was said.
The position of the guests around the table was determined by a hierarchy of the right to seek warmth: closest to the *stufa* sat the head of the family or the guest of honor, followed by the other members of the family in order of their importance. The women were responsible for the fire. After lighting it by striking a *pietra focaia* or flint, it was their job to make sure it never went out.
To retain as much of the heat from the stove as possible, the *stube*'s walls were covered with wood. As the material is sensitive to temperature and humidity, the boards were joined together without nails or screws to allow them to expand and shrink. The aesthetics of the *stube* would evolve over the centuries, sometimes following European fashions, but a little behind the times.
The earliest, Romanesque *stube* had a vaulted ceiling of an almost monastic

In Nicola Giol's Ca' dei Fiori, the old Tyrolean shiny green ceramic stove is set in a classic *stube* lined entirely with wood

simplicity, made of horizontal boards the same length as the walls and connected at the corners by a joist. The doors and windows were very small, and splayed to let in the light without losing too much warmth. The bench and table had sober lines.

The fourteenth century and Gothic period were to have a lasting influence on the style of the *stube*. It was adorned with columns, while the ceiling was given a gentler curve, with a large load-bearing beam in the middle. Ceilings with three small vaults appeared, and were decorated with carvings in geometric shapes. The windows grew slimmer and more elegant.

In the fifteenthth century the interiors became more richly decorated, the ceiling was made completely flat, and painted doors and baseboards were introduced. The furniture was transformed, and the first shelves were hung on the walls.

The sixteenth century saw the introduction of coffered ceilings and flat columns on the walls, while capitals in a classical style replaced the Gothic ones.

The volumes and motifs would reach the height of perfection in the seventeenth century.

Farmers and simply country folk who inherited a *stube* would never modify it but keep it as a relic of the past. Except in the event of fire, they were never destroyed but dismantled and then reassembled as they were moved from one home to another.

Two examples of masonry stoves. Left, the stove is framed by the wooden structure of the bed set on top and the benches covered with brightly colored fabrics; right, in the home of the artist Alice Mocellin, the stove passes through the wall and heats two rooms: the kitchen and a bedroom

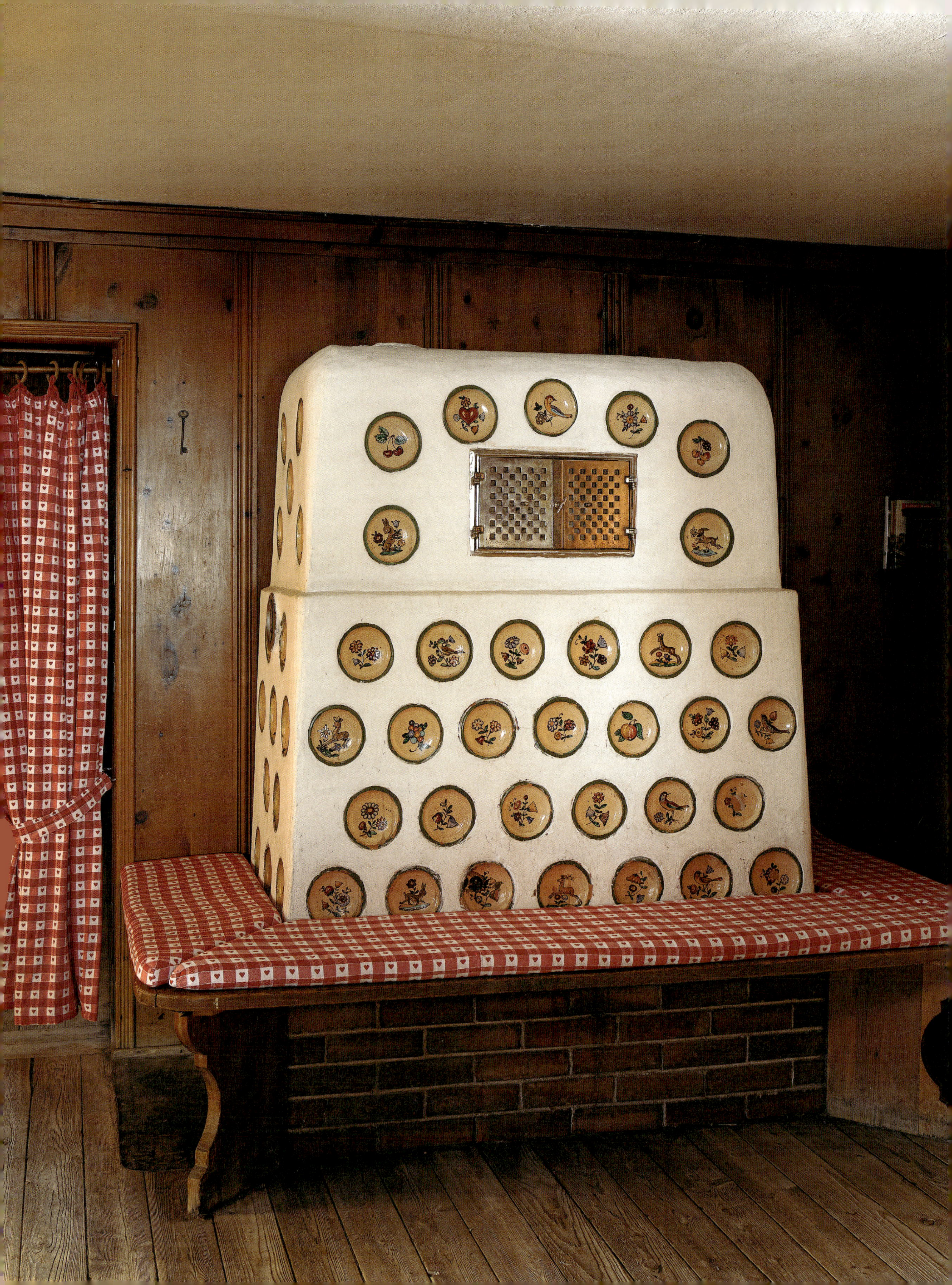

The *stube* is the setting for the *stufa*. These stoves, unlike traditional open fireplaces with large chimneys, are able to retain heat for long periods of time, letting it out slowly.
Of ancient origin, traces of them can be found from as far back as 1240. Around 1500 they began to be adorned for purely aesthetic reasons with ceramic tiles, molded or painted with flowers and animals by specialized craftsmen.
Due to seasonal migrations, the young artisans would spend time on prosperous farms in Bavaria, from where they returned with new ideas. Change took place slowly so as not to offend the elders, but little by little the *stube* were transformed. Thus in the thirteenth century the terracotta stoves in the Alpine valleys were given ceramic or majolica claddings, turning the *stufa* from a domestic appliance into a piece of furniture. In short, they became objets d'art.
It is possible to distinguish two main styles: the *Kachelöfen*, a vertical stove which can sometimes exceed two meters in height, covered entirely with finely decorated white or green ceramic tiles.
*Bauernöfen* for their part, are more modest masonry stoves. They are horizontal and take up a lot of room. They were usually filled with wood from outside the house. The stove was surrounded by a wooden structure called an *Ofenbank* or *banch da fornèl*: a sort of bench on which people would sit or lie to warm themselves. A cot for the baby was often placed above the stove.
Stoves are still the showpieces of any interior in Cortina. In the 1950s and '60s ,more modern ones were created by Edoardo Gellner, who liked to design not only their form but also the patterns of the tiles with which they were clad, introducing new production techniques and making their surface more shiny. The best known of these is the one that can be seen in the home of the Menardi family in *The Pink Panther* movie.

*left*
A large masonry stove decorated with ceramic dishes in a style typical of the mountains in the Counts Orsi Mangelli's Baita dell'Orso

*below and following pages*
Two ceramic stoves richly decorated in shades of blue. Below, the stove in Ca' del Rite bears the date 1793; the stove on the following pages dominates the dining room of Nicola Giol's Ca' dei Fiori

*previous pages*
In the wooden *stube* brought from Austria and reassembled in this house in Cortina, the Tyrolean green ceramic stove lends a touch of color to the room

In furnishing her home, Alessia Bianchi Bormioli has chosen to have the ceramic stoves play a leading part

# WINTER ANIMALS

## CORTINA AND THE BEAR

In the folk tradition of the Alps, the bear is often associated with wisdom and strength. There are numerous painted or sculpted images of bears, and it is easy to project human attitudes onto this animal in a humorous manner, giving it a friendly character. A whole series of pieces of furniture—benches, coatracks, umbrella stands—have been created that represent bears and their cubs. These massive and sturdy carved wooden objects are lumped under the name of the "Black Forest style." While the name comes from the homonymous mountainous region in western Germany, always a natural habitat of the bear, it seems that the origin of these objects and items of furniture lies in Switzerland, to be precise in the village of Brienz.

In the nineteenth century, the craftsmen of this region developed a rich production of furniture in the image of its fauna and flora, the animals and trees of its forests, made out dark brown or black wood. Other objects were no exception and were decorated with branches of trees, owls, and rabbits. The Black Forest style reached its peak between the late nineteenth century and the year 1910. Cortina succumbed to the craze and many chalets had furniture in this style. The popularity of the animal means that it is not uncommon to find its name on the doors of houses, the most iconic being La Baita dell'Orso which we see at the beginning of the film *Vacanze di Natale* (Carlo Vanzina, 1983). In 1988, Jean-Jacques Annaud chose the Dolomites as the setting for his film *The Bear*, the story of an orphaned bear cub which was a huge commercial success.

While a few, rare specimens of the animal have been seen in the Dolomites, the valley's most famous bear wandered for over thirty years around the center of Cortina, delighting adults and frightening the children who were photographed with him. Every family living in or passing through Ampezzo has in its album a photo of the white (but sometimes brown) bear of Cortina d'Ampezzo, a two-legged teddy bear which was an attraction on the Corso from the 1950s to the 1970s.

*left and following pages*
A coat rack with the figure of a bear in Black Forest style can be found in many of the valley's homes. These pages present various examples, also used as umbrella stands, walking stick and snowshoe racks, or hat stands

*left*
A wooden sculpture of a bear in the home of Chiara and Amedeo Reale

*this page*
The only bear ever seen in Cortina was on the Corso and remained there for thirty years. It is portrayed here in family snapshots. Above, the jeep that used to take skiers to the slopes in the 1950s, when there were still no ski lifts. Giovanna and Filippo Cordova, Donà dalle Rose, Zeno archives

*following pages*
In this house with an evocative name, the Counts Orsi Mangelli's Baita dell'Orso, or "Chalet of the Bear," the animal appears in various paintings used to decorate the walls and even on a fireplace in one of the bedrooms

## HORNED BEASTS: HUNTING AND THE ANIMALS OF AMPEZZO

In his *Cronaca*, Pietro Alverà writes that "in 1831 Pietro Alverà Dipol and Andrea Ghedina di Giustina killed the last bear in their sheep pen in Valbona. In 1845, the last wolf was seriously wounded by Giuseppe Zardini del Fauno. These wild animals have not been seen in Ampezzo for centuries." Large predators such as wolves, which became extinct in the Ampezzo Valley two centuries ago, have recently been reappearing in the localities of Cadin and Chiave and traces of bears can occasionally be found, but they are not considered a danger to people.

Animals have always been hunted by the inhabitants of the mountains for food or in order to defend their grazing herds. Hunting viewed as an adventurous challenge did not come until later, toward the end of the nineteenth century, when hunting permits started to be handed out, first to Count Melchiorri in 1873 and then to the Irish-Americans Emily Howard Bury and Anna Power Potts. Today the eighty-six members of the Riserva di Caccia di Cortina see themselves rather as guardians of the territory, with duties like replenishing the feeders and salt licks in winter and recording the number of animals.

Hunting has been subject to legal restrictions for a long time. As far back as 1815 the town council levied a tax on hoofed animals, with the forester responsible for its supervision.

*top*
The ballroom of Valcastello at Dobbiaco is decorated with numerous hunting trophies, symbols of the passion of the parents and grandparents of its present owner

*right*
The wooden façade of Paolo and Giuliana Clerici's house is decorated with sculptures of animal's heads with large antlers

Local Tyrolean superstitions would prove the greatest threat to deer, as they included the attribution of medicinal properties to powdered antlers.

The archbishop of Salzburg, Guidobald of Thun, demanded that his subjects bring him ibex horns, triggering a hunt that would lead to the slaughter of entire herds. It was the beginning of trade in the horns, and poaching of the animals. To stave off useless scuffles between hunters, the next archbishop of Salzburg ordered the extermination of all the ibex in the Tyrol mountains.

Another sad cause of the decline in the number of animals was the First World War. This brought about a tragic situation in which the resident fauna was almost completely wiped out due to a lack of food. Hunting would be banned for eight years, and the primary goal of the association of hunters set up in Cortina in 1920 was to restock the wildlife of the mountains.

Chamois and roe deer were reintroduced from other parts of the Alps. Attempts were made to introduce mouflon as well, but without success. In 1955, red deer reappeared, and in 1965 ibex were introduced into the Sorapiss area, from where they moved spontaneously toward the Hohe Gaisl.

Hunting continued along traditional lines until 1992, the year Italy passed a new law limiting the number of hunters. Hunting seasons were established for the first time by the province of Belluno, and the capercaillie and marmot were given the status of protected species.

In the 1960s, a terrible outbreak of strongylosis decimated the chamois, leading eventually to a ban on their hunting in 2005.

There are now only a few thousand roe deer in the Dolomites, along with small numbers of chamois.

Every year after the mating season, red and roe deer lose their antlers, which take three months to grow back. Their size varies according to age and diet. The collection of these antlers is legal and widespread, as it is highly profitable. In fact they are no longer sought for their medicinal properties but for their use in interior decoration. The material is also made into all kinds of objects, from knives and forks to frames and handles.

Trophies are often to be found hanging on the outside walls of barns. These should not be confused with shed antlers that have been collected. They are hunting trophies. Both the head and its antlers will be mounted on a wooden support and put on display in memory of the prowess of this or that hunter.

Taxidermy, that is to say the stuffing of an animal, preserves the whole of its body, along with its feathers or fur to make it look as alive as possible. Stuffed foxes, owls, capercaillies, and other birds are often found in Cortina d'Ampezzo. Very popular at the beginning of the last century for display in cabinets of curiosities, the taxidermy of protected species is prohibited today but legal for animals hunted with a permit.

*left*
A sculpture of a roebuck dominates Osanna Visconti's living room. Even the leather-topped stools have legs made from shed antlers

*above*
Hunting trophies on the walls of the dining room in a house at Chiave

Stags play a prominent role in this residence decorated by Jacques Grange. Guests are greeted by a metal stag in the garden and by a large wooden sculpture representing the same animal in the entrance

Two examples of the reuse of shed antlers as chandeliers. Left, in the dining room of Franco Toffoletto and Maurizia Villa; right, in the dining room of Paola Caovilla's home in Cortina designed by Luigi Vietti

## *LUSTER*

The most extraordinary object made out of antler in Tyrol is called a *luster*.
As its name implies, these are lamps and light fixtures carved out of the material and skillfully decorated.
They represent strange creatures, half-man and half-animal, whose legs end in antlers. There are no limits to their variety and shape, which are limited only by thwe imagination of the artisan who makes them.
We find the figures of men (hunters, climbers, musicians, innkeepers) as well as women (mermaids, young or mature beauties).
The lamps are generally hung from the ceiling above the traditional square Tyrolean table and its four chairs, but can also be used to decorate the central ceiling rose of the *stube*, as at the Hotel de la Poste.

A wall lamp representing a countrywoman and, right, a man playing a recorder that serves as a coat hanger

*following pages*
A *luster* in the form of an innkeeper hangs from the ceiling in the home of Paola Caovilla and another with a blacksmith decorates a coffered ceiling at the Hotel de la Poste

# WINTER MATERIALS

*left*
The typical façade of an Ampezzo home, built half of masonry and half of wood

*following page, left*
The wooden façade of the Sci Club 18's clubhouse

*following page, right*
The curved wooden back of Ca' Alleluia designed by Gaetano Rebecchini in the 1960s

## WOOD

A distinctive feature of houses in the Ampezzo Valley is that they are built half of stone and half of wood.
The south-facing stone part is reserved for the home, while the wooden part at the rear is used as a shelter for animals and for the storage of hay.
Wood (fir or larch) is used to ensure aeration of the hay to prevent it from rotting. The openings in the wood (*buje*) are also an expression of the carpenter's skill, as are the finely worked and carved balustrades. These barns (*fienili*) are considered fine works of carpentry. For the men of the mountain villages, becoming a woodcutter or woodworker was an obvious choice. The Alpine valleys developed a great tradition of woodworking (*falegnameria*), with the mountains offering different species of conifer—pines, firs, cirms—each with its own color and scent. Families had a personal sign with which they marked firewood and timber for construction: these famous *segni di casa* were handed down from father to son. At the heart of the house, the wooden *stube* or *stüa* symbolized the mastery of carpentry on the part of its proprietor: he was often the one who adorned it with capitals, friezes, and the *campo*, the large rose at the center of the ceiling.

18

Finally, the furniture, like the *stube*, was characteristic of the houses of Tyrol and Ampezzo. The variety and richness of its decoration means that an expert eye is immediately able to recognize its origin.
These pieces of furniture are also made of wood. From the *cassone* to the *cassapanca*, essential for the storage of clothing, their style evolved from Romanesque to Gothic and then Baroque. Typical are the seats around the table, the bench (*panca*), and then four-legged chairs with carved backs, decorated with masks, snakes and two-headed eagles, or with a generally heart-shaped opening.
Until the end of the Middle Ages, furniture was made by the carpenters responsible for building houses, with the help of such ancient crafts as woodturning or woodcarving. The emergence of the craft of joinery brought an acceleration in regional differentiation, with the Alpine regions preferring pine and fir. Joiners learned to use different types of wood for different purposes: maple or apple was good for veneer, while the best varieties for turning were basswood and cherry, and birch for marquetry. By the Renaissance, in fact, the production of furniture was no longer a matter of local knowhow but of high craftsmanship, and marquetry, entailed the combination of several kinds of wood to create ornamental patterns.
Other common designs were religious symbols, such as the monograms of Jesus and Mary or the crown of thorns surrounded by hearts. Initials were used to indicate the owners of the furniture, often accompanied by the date of their wedding when the furniture was part of a bride's trousseau. And the chest containing this trousseau, was the most important part. After the ceremony, the bride and her trousseau were carried to their new home on a cart adorned with garlands of flowers. It was a solemn procession in which everyone in the village took part. The contents of the chest always remained the property of the woman. Peddlers would spread Tyrolean furniture throughout the valleys, while the artisans of Cortina specialized in another type of woodworking: Tarkashi.

*left*
The dining room lined entirely with richly carved wood in Anna Marzotto's home

*below*
Detail of carved wooden columns

*following pages*
Many of the rooms in Nicola Giol's home, decorated by Tito Lebreton, are given a warm ambience by richly carved wood

*previous page, left*
A wooden ceiling carved by Giuseppe D'Incà

*previous page, right*
A dining table made from an old carved ceiling rose in Casa Modulo

*these pages*
Marvelous old doors salvaged and installed in the home of the architects Stefano Gris and Silvia Dainese

*following page, left*
The entrance of this house still has its original floor of square wooden blocks

*following page, right*
A typical scissors chair is juxtaposed with the modernity of sandblasted concrete and black beams with a charred effect in the home of the architects Stefano Gris and Silvia Dainese

*previous pages*
A magnificent row of old Ampezzo chairs
with their typical fretwork backs

Ampezzo fretwork chairs were used
in every room. Here they furnish
the kitchen in Nicola Giol's Ca' dei Fiori
and the dining room of Casa Zangrando

ZABOV
NONINO

Another Tyrolean specialty found in Ampezzo are the inlaid chairs; some of them would conceal a musical device in the seat

*following pages*
Architects and interior designers have fun today reinterpreting traditional wooden staircases. Left, a design by Studio Gris Dainese; right, a staircase in Alessia Bianchi Bormioli's home

## TARKASHI

In 1881, an Englishman called John Coddington introduced to Cortina a woodworking technique from the Mainpuri region of India that he had discovered on a journey made in the retinue of the Prince of Wales.

So it was that from the end of the nineteenth century Cortina d'Ampezzo became famed for the skill displayed by the practitioners of this craft. The Englishman had taught it to a local, Giuseppe Lacedelli, who went on to teach the craft at Cortina's Art School, laying the foundations for a tradition that would prove a great success.

Tarkashi is a technique of inlay that differs from traditional methods by inserting wire into the wood. The materials used are ebony and rosewood and the wire is made from zinc, copper, and brass. Small channels are cut with a chisel into the wood to accommodate strips of metal no wider than 2 or 3 mm. In Ladino, tarkashi is called *peta inze* (beating in,) in reference to the gesture made by the artisans.

Sometimes the surface of the wood is made more precious by the insertion of mother-of-pearl or silver, which is then polished. Tarkashi can be applied to all sorts of objects, from jewelry caskets to frames, plates, and even chairs.

This Oriental technique of inlaying wood has been preserved by a handful of artisans in the Ampezzo region, including Dario Menardi up until 2003, and is still practiced today by Ingrid Siorpaes.

Examples of tarkashi in two private collections; left, in Casa Gris Dainese; right, in the home of the antiquarian Claudio Zanettin

## THE *CHOPE*, BEER TANKARDS

Beer tankards provide an amusing testimony to the time when Cortina was part of the Austrian state of Tyrol. According Johann Heinrich Zedler in his *Grosses vollständiges Universal-Lexicon* (published in Leipzig between 1732 and 1750 and later cited in Meredith Chilton, Claudia Lehener-Jobst, *Fired by Passion*, 2009), beer had been a common drink in northern European countries since the seventeenth century. In fact the consumption of this drink has been very popular in northern European countries since the 17th century.
It is consumed by all walks of life, men and women alike. Craft breweries thrive and the vessels used vary from region to region depending on local traditions. Custom dictates that this is one of the traditional farewell gifts for a soldier from his regiment.*
A tankard is the name for a large mug used for drinking beer. It is a cylindrical cup with a handle that makes it easier to hold. Tankards could be found on all German and Austrian tables, from that of the emperor to that of the smallest mountain village. The only difference lay in the material from which the mug was made: silver, horn, pewter, terracotta, or fine porcelain.
In Goethe's language, the name varies from region to region, with several used interchangeably: *Mass,* meaning measure, a metric term replacing the old one of pint, or *Humpen, Seidel, Krug,* or *Walzenkruge* in the north. In English it is also known as a beer stein, a word borrowed from German.
These tankards or steins are sometimes fitted with a lid, called a *Zinndeckel* in German. Its origin seems to date back to the great outbreaks of plague in the fourteenth century, when the German Empire ordered all vessels containing food to be covered in an attempt to stem the disease. Lids made of tin proved useful as a defense against insects, dust, and above all heat, and have been preserved up to the present day. The tankard's lid can be more or less richly decorated. Failure to close it after taking a drink is inevitably viewed as a reason to pay for the next round.
The tankards themselves have a wide variety of decorations, ranging from noble coats of arms to simple motifs of flowers or fruit, sometimes carved in relief. The most precious example conceal a scene in the transparent bottom of the mug, only visible when it is emptied.
In the Tyrol they were often decorated with traditional motifs, such as mountain scenes, characters from folklore, and local symbols. They are very popular with collectors in Cortina for their unique aesthetic. There are even some that are specifically designed for men with mustaches!

*right and following pages*
In the home of a collector of old beer tankards of various materials, periods and origins

"BEER IS INDISPENSABLE [...]. IN THE NORTHERN AND EASTERN PARTS OF EUROPE, THE MOST IMPORTANT FOOD THAT MAN CONSUMES IS BEER [...] WHICH NOURISHES THE BODY AND MAKES IT FERTILE"

Johann Heinrich Zedler, cited in *Fired by Passion*, 2009

MICH AVS VND SCHENCK

*top*
At the Counts Orsi Mangelli's Baita dell'Orso, old beer tankards decorate the large fireplace

*right*
An original collection of pottery beer tankards in Nicola Giol's Ca' dei Fiori

*PL*
*ST*

*these and following pages*
In the home of Chiara and Amedeo Reale ceramic plates adorn the walls and play a primary role at table

# MOVIES AND WRITERS

## A SNOW-COVERED SET

The campanile in the snow, sleighs drawn by elegant horses, the little blue train of the Dolomites... Shortly after the first films set in the mountains, which focused mainly on climbing, Italian cinema started to take an interest in the Queen of the Dolomites' photogenic qualities in winter, exploiting the town's popularity following its hosting of the Olympic Games in 1956.
This is what led to the release of *Il conte Max* (*Count Max*, by Giorgio Bianchi) in 1957. A film that has since become a legend, it initiated a new genre of movies about winter vacations in Cortina. The iconic actor Alberto Sordi is a comical Roman newsagent who dreams of meeting the high society of the day and going on vacation to this swanky ski resort, while Vittorio De Sica plays his Pygmalion, the impoverished count. The stars of the film are Cortina d'Ampezzo's railway station and the Miramonti Majestic Grand Hotel.
The year 1959 saw the triumph of Camillo Mastrocinque's *Vacanze d'inverno* (Winter holidays). The same actors starring in a comedy with portraits of characters drawn from all levels of society, from a bored countess to a middle-class woman neglected by her husband. This movie would inspire the Vanzina brothers' *Vacanze di Natale* (Christmas holidays) in 1983. Something that was acknowledged by Enrico Vanzina in the book *Set in Cortina*: "Our foray into Cortina was a sincere homage to a genre that with *Vacanze d'inverno* produced what in my view is an amazing movie" (Enrico Vanzina in Ludovica Damiani, *Set in Cortina*, 2010.)
In an echo of the comic tropes of *Vacanze d'inverno*, the film features loud Romans, Milanese posers, and cheated wives or husbands. It was an infallible recipe and gave rise to the term *cinepanettone*, i.e. a commercially oriented comedy movie to be watched by the whole family while eating a panettone, the traditional Italian Christmas fruitcake. New versions of the "Christmas Holidays" movie would be shot in Cortina again in 2000 and in 2011.

*left*
The campanile in the snow
in a photograph from the 1920s/'30s.
Zeno archive

International recognition of Cortina d'Ampezzo would come in 1963 with Blake Edwards's *The Pink Panther*, the first in a series of films whose success is undeniable and which saw the birth of a legendary character, Inspector Clouseau. Against a snowy backdrop, shot mainly between the Hotel Cristallo and Casa Menardi (home of the hotel's owners), international thieves, Indian princesses, and a detective from the Paris police are bent on outwitting each other.

All the protagonists of a global jet set in Cortina that sparkles with the glamour of the movie's stars, David Niven, Claudia Cardinale, and Capucine.

The interiors of the film were shot in a studio in Rome, with a faithful reconstruction of the tavern built by the architect Edoardo Gellner for the Menardi family in 1947, with its distinctive stone-and-wood fireplace, as well as the hunting trophies on the wall. The actors knew this place well, dining there almost every evening. David Niven used to wear satin slippers so as not to damage the precious floor made of larch boards.

*above*
Robert Wagner and Capucine in *The Pink Panther* by Blake Edwards (1963)

THE *PINK PANTHER* CHALET

Casa Menardi, now the property of Silvia Iliceto, was built by the architect Edoardo Gellner in 1949. It was the famous specialist in mountain architecture's first building in Cortina and in 1963 it was chosen as a set for the first Pink Panther movie.
A decidedly avant-garde work of architecture, it has a tavern with a separate entrance that was intended to entertain the most distinguished guests. Under the eyes of the trophies hanging on the wall, the bag of that day's hunt would be cooked over the fire: haunches of venison, chamois...
The details of this room reflect Edoardo Gellner's deep knowledge of traditional mountain houses: the larch planking of the floor and the wrought iron of the doors are based on medieval models. Thus the furniture and decoration form part of an indivisible spatial whole in the room's interior design.

In 1981 it was the turn of the James Bond blockbuster *For Your Eyes Only* by John Glenn. Roger Moore played the famous spy, with Carole Bouquet as the Bond girl.
The great interest stirred by the Winter Olympics at Lake Placid in 1980 prompted the film's producers to choose a former Olympic site and a sports-related storyline. Cortina stood out for its facilities, such as the ski jump, biathlon stadium, skating rink, and in particular its magnificent bobsled track. In the film, James Bond skis down the Olympic piste of the Tofana, but it was actually his stuntman, the 1966 slalom champion Giovanni Dibona, who took the risk of hurtling down this steep run.
The real challenge of filming in winter remained a lack of snow. While James Bond's crew dealt with the problem by sending six or seven trucks every evening to collect snow from neighboring Austria (Mara Blasetti in Ludovica Damiani, *Set in Cortina*, 2010), Carlo Vanzina's crew came up with a more playful solution, resorting to a foam which stuck to the soles of their shoes for days at a time... It's a problem that filmmakers no longer face today thanks to the new special effects. The Christmas holidays have been saved!
And humor too. In 1993 it was the actor Paolo Villaggio as the star of *Fantozzi in paradiso* (*Fantozzi in Heaven*, by Neri Parenti) who, following in the footsteps of Totò and Peppino De Filippo, joined the long list of comic actors taking on the challenge of Cortina.

A CHAMPION ON SET

Giovanni Dibona was born in Cortina d'Ampezzo on March 12, 1944.
A champion slalom skier, he won two gold medals in 1966 and a bronze in 1969. He has been awarded the bronze medal for athletic prowess by the Italian Olympic Committee.
In 1981 he was Roger Moore's stuntman in the Bond movie *For Your Eyes Only*.

*bottom*
A set photo from the movie *For Your Eyes Only*

“CORTINA D'AMPEZZO, ONE OF THE CHOICEST RESORTS IN THE ALPS»

David Niven, *The Moon's a Balloon*, 1972

# "CHRIST, BUCK, THIS IS WONDERFUL COUNTRY [...] WE ARE TREATED LIKE ROYALTY AND WE ALWAYS HAVE A GOOD TIME"

Letter to his friend Buck Lanham in Carlos Baker, *Ernest Hemingway: A Life Story*,1969

Ernest Hemingway's room at the Hotel de la Poste. As well as the original furniture, some of the writer's personal belongings have been preserved, including his typewriter and a photo of him with a dedication

*following pages*
The bar of the Hotel de la Poste where Hemingway spent many evenings and which was his favorite place to meet up with Fernanda Pivano

## ERNEST HEMINGWAY IN CORTINA

It was in the early spring of 1923 that the "old Veneto Boy," as he liked to call himself, discovered Cortina d'Ampezzo in the company of his first wife, Hadley Richardson. It was there that he wrote the short story "Out of Season," which has a markedly autobiographical character. From the account of a young American couple on vacation in the Dolomites, between illegal fishing trips and a guide who drinks a bit too much, emerges the portrait of a young woman with a character very similar to Hadley's.

After this springtime visit, it was in winter that Hemingway, an excellent skier, would next return to Cortina.

Pregnant with their son Jack, who would be nicknamed Bumby, in 1924, Hadley got her doctor to give her permission to go skiing on condition that she took care not to fall...

In *A Moveable Feast* Hemingway describes how: "We all knew the different snow conditions and everyone knew how to run in deep powder snow" (Ernest Hemingway, *A Moveable Feast*, 1964).

This time the couple stayed at the Hotel Concordia and Ernest soon discovered the American bar at the Hotel de la Poste, haunt of all the local celebrities of the time, from the princes of the House of Fürstenberg to Hadley's lifelong friend, the pianist Renata Borgatti.

Grappa and Valpolicella flowed freely at the bar of the Hotel de la Poste, scene of some memorable evenings. The bartender had developed a brand new cocktail inspired by the Bellini of Venice, calling it Puccini in homage to the famous Tuscan composer and replacing peach juice with mandarin juice. Bumby took his first steps there in 1925, but the couple separated soon after and it was not until the late 1940s that Ernest Hemingway was seen in Cortina again.

In 1948, with a new wife in tow, his fourth and last, Mary Welsh, and a new Italian publisher for the translations of his books, the young Mondadori, he rented the Villa Aprile in Salieto, a charming chalet owned by Signora Palma Aprile from Milan.

The signing of the rental contract for the villa (paid by Mondadori out of his royalties) was celebrated at La Genziana in the company of his new friends the Kechlers, Robilants, and Franchettis, and above all two people who were to become his inseparable friends: Ettore Sottsass and Fernanda Pivano.

In fact it was in Cortina that Hemingway's decisive meeting with his Italian translator Pivano took place. It would prove to be a true friendship, at a personal and professional level, cemented during long drives aboard the blue Buick convertible, its boot well-stocked with bottles of gin, from the Passo delle Tre Cime di Lavaredo to Toblach and Bruneck, or even through the marvelous Val Badia while discussing Flaubert and Maupassant...

Hemingway's routine in Cortina was invariable: the mornings were taken up with writing sessions that the Pivano would recall with nostalgia in an article published in the *Corriere della Sera* in 1997: "Those hours from 5 to 11 were the best for those who could get close to him; you found out all about the way he wrote,

the way he thought, the way he suffered" (Fernanda Pivano, "A Cortina", in *Corriere della Sera*, 1997)
This was the time when paparazzi had started to appear on the scene. Journalists and photographers congregated under the larch trees of the Villa Aprile, but at this moment prior to the Olympic Games of 1956, Cortina was still a long way from the frenzy of the 1960s. After his writing sessions, "Papa" would go to Pocol to drink hot chocolate and above all to ski.
Hemingway was one of the first writers to talk, and especially to write about this sport of skiing, a relatively recently introduction in Italy. In *A Moveable Feast* he describes the advice given by the doctor to his pregnant wife when she wanted to go skiing. And in a letter to his friend John Dos Passos he expressed his disapproval of the new cable cars, which he said made people weak and lazy.
This letter followed an accident in which his wife Mary broke her ankle and had to be rushed to the Codivilla hospital...
In 1950, Hemingway moved into Room 107 at the Hotel de la Poste, where he finished his novel *Across the River and into the Trees*. Today his room has survived miraculously intact. Every piece of furniture is in its original place, including his typewriter, carefully preserved by the owners of the hotel. The ultimate mark of recognition is provided by the words he wrote in the register: "At the Hotel de la Poste we have been happy," signed Mary and Ernest Hemingway.
He would cherish these happy memories right up until the end. On July 1, 1961, the day before he died, he was still humming an Alpine tune he had learned from his friend Nanda, as he called Fernanda Pivano.

## PUCCINI COCKTAIL

*It's said that the Puccini cocktail, the winter version of the more famous Bellini, was invented in the late 1940s, when a barman called Renato Hausmann had the great idea of mixing mandarin juice and champagne for a drink with a fresh and lively taste. It was in 1948 at the Hotel de la Poste in Cortina d'Ampezzo that this cocktail was served for the very first time.*

- *cocktail or flute glass*
  *directly in a chilled glass*
- *4 oz. (12 cl) sparkling wine*
- *3 oz. (9 cl) freshly squeezed and filtered mandarin juice (alternatively clementine juice)*
- *decorate with mandarin (clementine), optional cherry, and mint leaf*

*above*
Ernest Hemingway in Cortina d'Ampezzo, 1949

# WINTER STYLE

"HE LOOKED ROUND AND SAW A SMALL ROUND WOMAN IN A WHITE MINK COAT LINED WITH DARK MINK. ON HER HEAD WAS A POINTED MILITARY CAP, ALSO OF WHITE AND DARK MINK, AND EVEN HER BOOTS WERE DECORATED WITH THE SAME WHITE AND DARK MINK, IN A HERRINGBONE PATTERN"

Goffredo Parise: "Hatred," in *Solitudes*, 1998

*left*
Sheepskins cover the seats in Anna Marzotto's living room

*following pages*
Warm couches welcome the guests in Osanna Visconti's lounge

## CORTINA AND FUR

The image is a vivid one, and is reminiscent of a now iconic picture of two women dressed in fur jackets and boots chatting in front of the Bredo Abbigliamento store in Cortina that was taken by the American photographer Slim Aarons in 1982. Fur is inseparable from the style of Cortina. It is the undisputed protagonist of strolls along the Corso in winter. It is found in all the movies set in the town, worn by both men and women.

There is nothing new about this. On September 19, 1991, the body of a hunter from the Chalcolithic Age emerged from the ice of the Val Senales in an exceptional state of preservation. Ötzi, as this ancestor of ours from 5300 years ago has been dubbed, is now in the South Tyrol Museum of Archaeology in Bolzano and is dressed entirely in fur and leather. The inner part of his coat is made of goatskin and sheepskin, worn with the fur on the inside. The shoes are made of goatskin, bound to an upper made of deer hide. As for his headgear, a sort of cap, it is made of strips of bearskin, with a leather chin strap attached to the lower edge, and can be regarded as an ancestor of the busby.

Ötzi's remains show that the fur of animals obtained from hunting has long been used for clothing. Over the course of time it came to be used for furnishings as well. Mountain communities frequently turned to animal fur to combat the cold in unheated rooms of the house. Today synthetic fur is taking the place of the real stuff. The second half of the twentieth century saw the birth of the *animalier* style, a fashion that imitated the patterns of the coat of various animals and reproduced them in faux fur. The fabrics would be used in clothing and in the home too. The interior designer Roland Terenzio, for example, made extensive use of it in a chalet in Cortina from the 1960s.

*previous page, left*
A view of Osanna Visconti's home

*previous page, right*
This living room presents several elements typical of Ampezzo, such as the coffered ceiling, the picture hung at an angle high on the wall, and the low wooden table with footrests at its base

In this large mansard, the French velvet with a leopard-skin print plays an essential part in the furnishings designed by Roland Terenzio in the 1960s

*below*
A corner of the living room in a house at Chiave

*right*
The veranda of Valcastello

LA DOLCE VITA
A CORTINA

Cowhide is often used in the furnishing of houses in the mountains, including as rugs and seat covers. In this case, on the left, an original covering for the desk in a home designed by Jacques Grange; below, at Valcastello

*following pages*
Various rooms in different houses are given a warm feel by the use of wool, boiled wool, felt, tartan, or floral fabrics

A
N

ME QUIERO

Typical winter decorations for outdoors
made from sprigs of pine leaves, pinecones,
and heather

An old cart and sled house decorations with dried flowers and heather in various colors in a house with an evocative name: Nicola Giol's Ca' dei Fiori or House of Flowers

*above*
The creation of floral decorations for the home is an old tradition among the women of the Ampezzo valley. Today, multicolored garlands and bouquets can be found at Cortina's florist, Ampezzan Fiori

*right*
An enchanting atmosphere in a corner of Nicola Giol's Ca' dei Fiori decorated by Tito Lebreton

*below*
A contemporary table setting that recalls the geometric forms of old coffered ceilings in Anna Marzotto's home

*right*
A Christmas table in a house in Cortina

*above*
Dried flowers, berries, and a collection of old pewter objects form an attractive centerpiece in Casa Alverà

*right*
A lounge in Casa Marzotto in the warm and unmistakable style of Luigi Vietti

*following pages*
The Christmas spirit is felt particularly strongly in the mountains. The lavish external decoration of Paola Caovilla's home and the big Christmas tree in another house are two examples

Ultimate Collector Cars
Ultimate Collector Cars

# COMFORT FOOD

## DISHES OF THE AMPEZZO VALLEY

A border town, Cortina's recipes bring together the flavors of Tyrol with those of Italy.
The most typical dish is undoubtedly *casunziei*, a type of stuffed pasta that has a red filling of beetroot in the winter and a green one of ricotta and wild herbs in the summer, both served with butter and parmesan cheese and sprinkled with poppy seeds. Delicious whatever the season.
Borrowed from the Veneto tradition, the ever-present polenta is served with mushrooms, fondue, and goulash.
From the Tyrolese tradition come *canederli*, large bread dumplings stuffed with cheese, speck, or spinach, and *spätzle*, small green or white egg noodles. And it is in desserts that the influence is strongest. The names speak for themselves: *Strudel, Kaiserschmarrn, Sachertorte, Krapfen, Linzer torte*. Cortina's numerous *pasticcerie* have perfectly mastered this historical legacy.
The valley does not have a wide variety of its own desserts. The one that is most symbolic of Cortina is *carafòi*: sweet crackers fried in oil, these were made for special occasions such as festivals, weddings, and baptisms, and are still commonly eaten at carnival time.
"*Carafòi* was a dessert that could be served on any occasion," according to Rachele Padovan in her book of local recepes.
After the First World War, the diet gradually became globalized, but traditional recipes have retained a strong presence in the local gastronomy.

*left*
The kitchen with a large masonry stove in Alice Mocellin's home

## WHITE *SPÄTZLE*

*White* spätzle *are a winter variant of the classical "green" ones made with spinach. People used to make them during the cold season when this vegetable didn't grow in the kitchen garden. In fact, ingredients such as flour, milk, eggs, onion, speck, and potatoes were plentiful in the pantry in the winter too.*

- *1 kg flour*
- *7 eggs*
- *600 ml fresh milk*
- *salt*
- *pepper*
- *dry breadcrumbs*
- *grated mature cheese*
- *browned butter*

*Take a bowl and mix the flour, eggs, milk, salt and, if available, some freshly ground black pepper with a large wooden spoon.*
*The mixture should be worked by hand for at least 10 minutes until it acquires a texture similar to fresh ricotta.*
*Put on a pot with salted water and using a special utensil called a* macinaspätzle *press a tablespoonful for each portion.*
*As soon as the water starts to boil again, add to the* spätzle *a handful of diced boiled potatoes.*

*Boil on high heat for 2 minutes and then use a strainer to delicately place the well-drained* spätzle *on a plate.*
*Sprinkle the* spätzle *with the grated cheese and breadcrumbs and serve with browned melted butter.*

Recipe from Claudio Alverà, Dolomiti Lodge, Alverà family

## CASUNZIEI

*Cortina's typical half-moon-shaped ravioli, in the version stuffed with beetroot.*

*For the pasta:*

- *300 gr flour*
- *2 whole eggs*
- *a pinch of salt*
- *water as needed*

*For the filling:*

- *5 beetroots*
- *1 turnip (or rutabaga) or 2 potatoes*
- *salt*
- *pepper*

*For the seasoning:*

- *butter*
- *Parmesan*
- *breadcrumbs*
- *poppy seeds*

*Put the flour on a pastry board and make a well in the center. Add the eggs, salt, and as much water as needed. Knead until smooth, cover with a dish towel and leave to rest for half an hour.*
*Boil the beetroot and turnips (or potatoes) and pass them through a vegetable mill. Pour the vegetables into a bowl and add a little flour browned in an iron saucepan, salt and pepper.*
*Roll out the dough into a thin sheet; cut out discs with a round pastry cutter, place the filling in the center and fold the disc to form a half-moon, pressing on the edge with the fingers.*
*Salt and boil the water and cook the* casunziei *for about 10 minutes.*
*Place on a serving dish and season with Parmesan cheese or zigar (a local cheese made from sour milk), breadcrumbs, browned butter, and poppy seeds.*

Recipe taken from Francesca Gaspari and Maria Luisa Menardi, *Coślùpe frite e lòchi 'n técia: Raccolta di ricette della tradizione ampezzana* (Cortina d'Ampezzo: no date).

## AMPEZZO POTATOES



*A simple recipe that flavors a dish of plain boiled potatoes with ingredients easy to obtain in the mountains.*

- *1 kg potatoes*
- *150 gr onion sliced into thin rounds*
- *80 gr speck cut into strips*
- *Vegetable oil as needed*

*Boil the potatoes, removing them from the heat 5 minutes before they are completely cooked, peel them and slice them into rounds. Heat vegetable oil in a skillet, add the potatoes and onions and when they start to turn golden brown add the speck. Sauté for another 3 minutes. Once served sprinkle with finely chopped chives.*

Recipe from Claudio Alverà,
Dolomiti Lodge, Alverà family

*left*
A corner of the kitchen in Casa Bianchi Bormioli

*following page, right*
An old wooden closet decorated with carvings of matrimonial scenes. This sort of closet was part of the bride's trousseau

## *BRAZOLÀ* (WEDDING CAKE)

*A week before their wedding, bride and groom used to go round to invite relatives and friends with a basket containing a* brazolà, *five* carafòi, *and five comfits. The first to be visited were their godfathers and godmothers, and then their relatives and friends.*
*The* brazolà *is a braided ring cake, strewn with granulated sugar, made in bakeries.*

- *500 gr flour*
- *80 gr sugar*
- *80 gr butter*
- *5 eggs*
- *zest of 1 lemon*
- *1 packet vanilla powder*
- *40 gr brewer's yeast*
- *80 gr milk*
- *salt*
- *granulated sugar for decoration*

*Combine all the ingredients in a bowl and mix in the yeast dissolved in a small amount of warm milk. Work the mixture for about half an hour and leave to rest for half an hour near a source of heat. Divide the mix into three parts and form them into a braid shaped into a ring. Leave to rest for half an hour again. Brush the top of the cake with egg yolk beaten with a little water and sprinkle with granulated sugar. Bake at 180°C for 30 minutes.*

Recipe taken from Francesca Gaspari and Maria Luisa Menardi, *Coŝlùpe frìte e lòchi 'n técia: Raccolta di ricette della tradizione ampezzana* (Cortina d'Ampezzo: no date).

A richly laid table for a winter afternoon snack with traditional Austrian desserts such as Sachertorte, strudel and Krapfen

CORTINA

# SUMMER

GUIDA ILLUSTRATA
DI
CORTINA
CARTA TURISTICA
DELLA ZONA DELLE
DOLOMITI

# HIKERS, CLIMBERS, AND HUNTERS

*left*
Old maps on waterproof oilcloth from the 1920s/'30s in the archive of Valcastello. The early trekkers used them on their walks even though they were always accompanied by a guide

## THE FIRST HIKERS AND CLIMBERS AND THE DAWN OF ROYAL TOURISM

The magnificent bowl of Cortina surrounded by its giants of stone has long been a delight for nature lovers, hikers, and climbers, with trails of great diversity suitable for all levels.

The very first hikers were the inhabitants of Cortina. They discovered their mountains on Sunday strolls with the family, armed with the traditional *Alpenstock*, a long stick with an iron spike at the tip onto which *Stocknageln*, small souvenir badges of the places they visited on foot, were nailed.

Due to their occupation, shepherds, hunters, and even poachers would prove to be mines of information for generations of climbers. Hunters, in particular, have an extraordinary sense of balance and great skill in finding passes through the mountains. As do those tireless hikers the topographers, often from the military.

Even though there was no mountaineering culture in Cortina until the middle of the eighteenth century, it was hiking and climbing that lay at the root of the phenomenon of tourism in Ampezzo. The first foreign visitors were British and would describe the beauty of the Dolomites in glowing terms, encouraging other Europeans to come and discover this valley, its lakes, and its mountains.

The first book was published by Walter White in 1855: *On Foot Through Tyrol: In the Summer of 1855*. It was followed in 1859 by John Ball's *Peaks, Passes, and Glaciers*, a pioneer of its genre.

In 1860, it was the artist Josiah Gilbert and the geologist George Cheetham Churchill who arrived in Cortina with their wives, publishing *The Dolomite Mountains* in 1865. Lucy Tuckett's *Zigzagging amongst Dolomites* was the next to come out, in 1871. Finally Amelia B. Edwards's excellent *Untrodden Peaks and Unfrequented Valleys* was published in 1873, a lavish account of her visits filled with anecdotes about the local economy. This literature, with its enthusiastic descriptions, would disseminate Cortina's reputation far and wide and soon a wealthy clientele began to flock to the first three hotels, established in 1877: Croce Bianca, La Stella d'Oro, and L'Aquila Nera with its pretty façade painted by the sons of its owner, Gaetano Ghedina.

It was at L'Aquila Nera that a key figure in mountaineering arrived by stagecoach in the middle of the summer of 1862: Paul Grohmann. He would begin a long series of climbs in the Dolomites, accompanied by the local guides Angelo Dimai, Francesco Lacedelli, and Santo Siorpaes. Before them, only a few adventurous Englishmen had attempted to conquer the peaks, such as Monte Pelmo, climbed by John Ball in 1857.

Everything changed with Grohmann and his companions, who set out to ascend each virgin peak systematically, conquering the Tofana di Mezzo in 1863, the Sorapis and Monte Cristallo in 1865, and the Tofana di Fuori in 1865.

This was the first phase of climbing in Cortina and would last until 1880: the conquest of all the major peaks would attract the attention of ever-growing numbers of people, with the challenge of the Dolomites luring European mountaineers and fascinating the locals, resulting in the creation of generations of guides. Cortina's first consortium of guides was set up in 1876, offering visitors over fifty routes to be followed on foot or horseback.

The second phase of mountaineering saw the conquest of all the minor summits. Every tower, spire, and steeple would be tackled until they had all been climbed. Then the third phase opened up increasingly difficult routes and trails, and in 1930 climbers succeeded in overcoming the dreaded grade 6.

The biggest change in mountaineering in the 1930s was that it entered the collective imagination of European society. Climbers became national heroes in Italy and Germany. The spectacular act of climbing and the majesty of the mountains propelled them onto the front pages of the international press, while medals were awarded to the most daring mountaineers. This kind of popularity was something completely new for climbers, who up until that time had attracted little attention.

The activity experienced enormous growth in a climate of competition which led to the first casualties, as the sheer number of climbers resulted in a fall in safety standards, exacerbated by the lack of expert guides. The fourth phase, which has lasted until the present day, has seen a return to free climbing, without the use of aids, conducted for reasons of personal satisfaction. Nowadays, Alpine tourism has changed a great deal: the trails are clearly signposted, dotted with hospitable refuges and *vie ferrate* accessible to all, while the role of guides has shifted towards teaching people respect for nature and safety.

*top*
Count Lorenzo Donà dalle Rose with his sons Nicolò and Luigino on a summer hike in the vicinity of Cortina, 1940s. Donà dalle Rose archive

*right*
In the home of a collector, a picture of the Ampezzo Valley in the summer painted by Edward Harrison Compton in 1908

## A KEY FIGURE: KING ALBERT I OF BELGIUM

Dubbed the mountaineer or climber king, Albert I declared more modestly: "I don't go mountain climbing, I take walks in the mountains."

It was in September 1908 that the young Albert, still a prince at the time (he was to ascend the throne the following year) discovered Cortina. In the company of the guides Angelo Dimai and Agostino Verzi, he made the ascent of several peaks with extraordinary success: Croda da Lago (2,715 m/8,907 ft) on September 28; Cima Piccola (2,856 m/9,370 ft) on September 29; Piz Popena (3,152 m/10,341 ft) on October 1; and Marmolada (3,343 m/10,968 ft) on October 5.

These remarkable achievements, which impressed his guides and caught the interest of the local community, marked the beginning of a long romance between the king and Cortina d'Ampezzo. Albert, who regarded climbing a fundamental experience for the human spirit, returned every year, sometimes climbing with his wife Elisabeth of Bavaria and their children, passing his love of Ampezzo on to them. The memory stayed with his son Leopold, who would spend long periods at the Hotel Argentina in Pocol with his second wife Lilian of Réthy and inherited his father's passion for climbing. One of the most demanding peaks in the eastern Alps is dedicated to Leopold: the Campanile di Brabante.

King Albert died on February 17, 1934, following a tragic climbing accident in Belgium. The Dolomites honored him by building a refuge named after him at an altitude of 2,621 m in the Rosengarten group, on the border between the Fassa Valley and South Tyrol.

But Albert's most lasting legacy in Cortina was in the person of his daughter Marie-José, who forged the link that brought the Royal House of Savoy back to Cortina.

On January 8, 1930, Marie-José married the heir to the Italian throne, the Prince of Piedmont, Umberto of Savoy, the future King Umberto II. It was in Cortina that the young couple, fresh from their honeymoon, made their first public appearance, and they were to return there often.

While Queen Margherita of Savoy had stayed at Misurina in 1900, Marie-José preferred the Savoy Hotel, which she patronized along with the other princesses of the House of Savoy, Giovanna, Yolanda, and Mafalda. Prince Umberto stayed at the Tre Croci Hotel, and would leave his mark on all the society events associated with sport and tourism in Cortina.

For over a hundred years, from the middle of the eighteenth century to the middle of the nineteenth, all the royal families of Europe passed through Cortina, including the Romanov princesses, the Duke of Genoa, and the families of the princes of Austria. Another member of the Italian royal family, Amedeo of Savoy-Aosta, was so popular in Ampezzo that, in 1938, Cortina's primary school, was named after him, as was a refuge on the Tofana where he often stopped to put on his crampons.

Duke Amedeo of Aosta, a fascinating man who was also known as the Iron Duke or the hero of Amba Alagi, was a frequent visitor to the valley. At dawn he could be found on the Tofana, which he used to descend at great speed, being an excellent skier. In the book *Cortina. Ritratto inedito di una signora*, he was described by Giovanni Nuvoletti Perdomini as

> "THE NEW AND AMAZING FORMS OF THESE COLOSSAL MOUNTAINS; THEIR STRANGE COLORING; THE MYSTERY OF THEIR FORMATION; THE SINGULARITY OF THEIR RELATIVE POSITIONS, EACH BEING SO NEAR ITS NEIGHBOR, YET IN ITSELF SO DISTINCT AND ISOLATED"

Amelia B. Edwards, *Untrodden Peaks and Unfrequented Valleys*, 1873



follows: "Solitary, strict, fraternal, he was the spur that drove us youngsters to venture each morning on daring exploits in the Dolomites."

The mountains had certainly long been a passion in the Aosta family. In 1909, Luigi Amedeo of Savoy, Duke of the Abruzzi, led the first Italian expedition to K2. He ventured into the heart of the Karakorum range with local guides and porters and the photographer Vittorio Sella. The duke's expedition failed to reach the summit but garnered a wealth of information that would prove vital to the success of future expeditions.

Twenty years later, his nephew Aimone of Savoy led another expedition, accompanied by the explorer Ardito Desio, to collect scientific data in the Karakorum. In the end it was an Italian expedition that included a climber from Cortina, Lino Lacedelli, a member of the Scoiattoli group of mountaineers, that ascended the summit of K2 on July 28, 1954. It was the beginning of the legend of the "Squirrels."

*page left, from the top*

King Umberto of Savoy's visit to Cortina in 1923. Private archive

Leopold of Belgium, middle, Carlo Franchetti, right, and a guide from Ampezzo Attilio Tissi, left, during the first ascent of the Campanile di Brabante, September 2, 1933. Franchetti archive

Amedeo of Aosta, right, and Carlo Franchetti in Cortina in the 1930s. Franchetti archive

*right*

Above this fireplace stands a picture of Cortina painted by an Austrian artist in 1885

## CORTINA SQUIRRELS

The group of climbers called the Società Scoiattoli (the Squirrel club) was formed in 1939 at the behest of some of the younger people of Ampezzo.

Set up on July 1, 1939, as Società Scoiattoli, it was soon renamed the Società Rocciatori e Sciatori Gli Scoiattoli (The Squirrel club of rock climbers and skiers) as all of its members were also expert skiers. It had ten founding members, for whom the only requirement was birth and residence in the Ampezzo valley. Its distinctive outfit, a red woolen sweater with a white squirrel on the left shoulder, would come to be worn by all the best mountaineers, and still is today.

At the time of the group's foundation, none of its members were as yet professional guides or climbers. The aim of these young "hotheads," as their elders saw them, was to learn safe climbing techniques, as those already working as guides were too busy to train them.

*The best known of the "squirrels" is probably Lino Lacedelli, who in 1954 unfurled the Scoiattoli flag on the highest peak of the Karakoram range, K2 (altitude 8,611 m/28,251 ft.)

The conquest of K2 was a race against time between teams from the United States, France, Germany, and even New Zealand.

The first American expeditions in 1938 and 1939 stopped at 7,900 m and 8,400 m respectively, the latter just 200 m below the summit. Quite a feat, nevertheless, given the time and the still rudimentary equipment.

On July 28, 1954, eleven Italian mountaineers began the final stage of their successful attempt on the mountain. Achille Compagnoni and Lino Lacedelli, who reached the summit thanks to the oxygen tanks carried to the last camp by Walter Bonatti and Amir Mahdi, a Pakistan climber, became national heroes, ensuring that the Scoiattoli group went down in history and propelling them into the limelight on the world stage.

The squirrel has become the symbol of Cortina, red for its mascot, silver for the tourism agency which used to give it each year as a reward to faithful visitors to the town (such as Princess Anna Corsini in 1994) and bronze in color for ski trophies. As for the white squirrel on a red background, it still flies over the resort's chalets, while the group continues its rescue activities.

*top*
The symbol of the squirrel has become Cortina's logo

*bottom*
First poster for *Gli Scoiattoli di Cortina*, 1939. At the center, portraits of the ten founding members. Archivio Scoiattoli di Cortina

*right*
A skiing trophy in the characteristic form of a squirrel

"THE TRADITIONALIST CIRCLES OF THE MOUNTAIN GUIDES IMMEDIATELY SHOWED MARKED HOSTILITY TOWARDS THE NEW GROUP [...] BUT THEY WERE SOON FORCED TO CHANGE THEIR OPINION IN THE FACE OF THE FIRST DIFFICULT BUT RESPONSIBLY CONDUCTED CLIMBS MADE BY THE *SCOIATTOLI*"

Giovanni Cenacchi, *Gli Scoiattoli di Cortina*, 1989

# THE CASTLES OF CORTINA

## A STRANGE TWIST OF FATE

All that is left today to bear witness to the three castles constructed in Cortina d'Ampezzo since the town's foundation are a few stones and some pleasant strolls... A rare occurrence and a mark of the valley's fairly democratic destiny.

## CASTELLO DI BOTESTAGNO (OR PODESTAGNO)

The earliest castle of which record can be found is called Bodestagno or Podestagno, from the German *Puiselstein* or *Boitestein* meaning "rock on the River Boite." It was a small medieval fort which stood on the mountain of the same name in the Valle del Boite, to the north of Cortina d'Ampezzo. The first document to mention its existence dates from 1175 and refers to a "Locus qui dicitur Botestain in Cadubrio." It was probably built by the Lombards in the seventh or eigth century with the aim of dominating the three valleys of the Valle del Boite, Val di Fanes and Val Felizon. From 1077 to 1420, the whole region was the property of the powerful Patriarchs of Aquileia, who in the thirteenth century made it a captaincy. Its strategic position on the road known as the Strada Regia di Alemagna, connecting the northeast of Italy with the Holy Roman Empire, allowed the patriarchs to exact a toll from the lords of da Camino and to provide merchants with a perfect place to break their journey.

In 1420, the entire region came under the control of the Republic of Venice, but this would last for only ninety years because in 1511 it was incorporated into Maximilian I of Habsburg's County of Tyrol.

It was at this point that the castle reached its apogee. Under the rule of the Habsburgs, a series of expansions took it to its definitive form. By this time it consisted of a three-story building with a chapel, dining halls, armory, prisons, and the heated rooms known as *stuben*...

In 1719, the change in trade routes brought about by the opening of the free port of Trieste resulted in a decline in Botestagno's importance, and in the eighteenth century the emperors of Austria ordered its abandonment. The last captain of the garrison, Franz von Winkelhofen, left in 1752.

*left*
One of the surviving towers of the Castello de Zanna

The municipality of Cortina bought what was left of the castle for three hundred florins and decided to demolish it, tearing its roof and lofts down in 1794 and demolishing it completely by 1867. A rare photo taken by Baron Nathaniel de Rothschild in 1865 shows the castle in ruins but still clearly visible. The reason for its destruction? Probably feelings of rancor... Having long suffered under its occupants, it is likely that the local population wanted to eliminate all trace of the fort and its commanders. Legend has it that part of the traditional costume worn by the women of Cortina, the famous *peza da sen*, or breast piece, was due to the need to make their necklines less visible to the lord of Botestagno since he was able to demand the *ius primae noctis*, or the right of this lord to sleep with betrotted women.
The little that remained of the castle's ancient walls was destroyed by Italian soldiers at the beginning of the First World War, when it was turned into an observation post for light artillery. On the 500th anniversary of the conquest of Ampezzo by Emperor Maximilian in 2011, the site was cleared and a campaign of archaeological excavations got under way. It is now easy to access the ruins by a pleasant walk.

## CASTELLO DE ZANNA: A CASTLE RESISTED

Toward the end of 1690, the nobleman Gianmaria de Zanna decided to build a castle, or rather a small fortress, at Majon. The dominant position and absence of houses in the vicinity made it an ideal location. Faithful to its tradition of equality and democratic principles, the community of Ampezzo did not look favorably on the construction of a fortified residence, and the work was halted in 1696 on the grounds that it was not consistent with the local constitution.
Out of this reluctance and consequent abandonment was born the legend of the workers destroying at night what they had built during the day.

A table setting on a hunting theme at Valcastello and the interior of an old cutlery drawer in Casa Zangrando

*following pages*
A collection of silver drinking cups with a hunting theme at Valcastello

In 1809, de Zanna Castle, in reality nothing more than a large unfinished house, was set on fire by the French troops who had invaded Ampezzo, destroying it. Only two towers, part of the outer walls, and the church dedicated to the Trinity survive. The walls originally surrounded the house and the church. The narrow path leading to the site has been turned into a proper road called the Via del Castello in memory of Gianmaria de Zanna's unfulfilled dream. It is still the property of his descendants.
An interesting site note: the Castel de Zanna and the Pomagagnon mountain group behind it were used as a symbol of Cortina on postcards dating from the beginning of the last century.

## "THE ENGLISHWOMEN'S HUNTING LODGE": CASTELLO DI SANT'UBERTO

Located near the Tornichè, this is perhaps the least known of Cortina's three castles, even though it is the most recent.
It was built at the behest of two women, whom people in Ampezzo commonly referred to as *le inglesi*, the English ladies (although in reality one of them was Irish and the other American). College friends and passionate about nature and hunting, they named the castle after Saint Hubertus, patron of hunters and foresters. Lady Emily Alfreda Julia Bury (Dublin 1856–Paris 1931) was the daughter of William George, third Earl of Charleville and owner of Charleville Castle at Tullamore in Ireland (a sumptuous property where Emily lived from 1875 and probably the source of her inspiration). Married to Kenneth Howard, she was widowed after just five years of marriage when her husband died at the age of thirty-nine.
Their son Charles Kenneth Howard-Bury spent long periods in Cortina. He had a marked taste for hunting and especially for climbing (he had shot a man-eating tiger that had killed twenty-one holy men in India and had explored the Tien Shan mountains of Tibet. Earning the rank of colonel in the British army during the First World War, he was made the leader of the Mount Everest reconnaissance expedition in 1921, which stopped short of the summit. Another little side note: the British press gave him the credit for discovery of the yeti, or abominable snowman, following his description of the tracks of what he believed to be a big grey wolf living at an altitude of 6,000 meters.
Thus the time he had spent in the Dolomites as a youth was to leave a deep mark on the rest of his life.
The second "Englishwoman," the heiress Anna Power Potts (Dublin 1866–Cortina 1906), was the former wife of Admiral Templin Morris Potts, governor of the island of Guam.
After spending a winter in Merano, the two friends decided to build the Castello di Sant'Uberto.
The application for a building permit was filed by Giovanni Apollonio and the architect Albert Burnley Bibb on March 24, 1897, at the request of the two foreign owners of the land. The design was for a small castle with two towers and two outbuildings, one for the servants and the other for the stables and carriages. Construction was swift, with the roof beams in place by the end of 1897. In its various reception rooms, *le inglesi* enetertained not just their friends but also members

of the local community, who quickly took to them tas a result of their generosity towards the poor children of Cortina d'Ampezzo.

The two friends were pioneers. It was a secluded spot, overlooking the whole of the Boite valley, but at the time only a few foreigners with a passion for science or geology ventured into the Dolomites. Gilbert and Churchill's book published in 1864 and Amelia B. Edwards's book from 1873 paint a fairly clear picture of the difficulty of reaching the Ampezzo valley in Tyrol at the time: few or no roads, and few or no side-saddles for women to ride the mules that were indispensable on mountain paths. The title of Edwards's book is significant: *Untrodden Peaks and Infrequent Valleys*. Twenty years after Amelia made the journey, a stagecoach service ran from Cortina to the railway line at Toblach, making access easier for the pair of "Englishwomen."

It was their love of the Dolomites and nature that enabled them to obtain the right to hunt on the many acres of their estate; a right they retained from 1898 to 1908, the year when the dream faded...

In 1906, Anna died suddenly. In the will she had drawn up on September 18, 1899, she left the property of theCastello di Sant'Uberto in the Ampezzo valley, Austria, to her dear friend Lady Emily Howard, on condition that she pass it on to Anna's son Templin Powers Potts when she died.

So great was her attachment to Cortina that her heart (or perhaps her ashes) was buried in a precious casket under the pine trees of the estate. When Italy entered the Great War in 1915 and attackedAustria, the castle was unlucky enough to be situated on the road to Toblach, at a strategic location for the Austro-Italian front.

The mansion would be stripped of its furniture and decorations... It is said that a grand piano ended up in the Austrian trenches. Since the Castello di Sant'Uberto was owned by a citizen of Ireland, and thus of a country that was still part of the British Empire at the time, and a citizen of the United States, soon to declare war against Austria-Hungary, it would be burned to the ground by the *Standschützen*. Emily left Cortina d'Ampezzo for good and would die in Paris in 1931.

The people of Cortina had been extremely fond of the two "Englishwomen," with their generosity to the poor and love of the area. In memory of her friend who had died too young, Lady Emily even presented the town with a sanatorium for tuberculosis patients. It was completed in 1909, but was never granted permission to begin operation. The countess then sold it to the Verzi family, who turned it into a hotel. The proceeds from the sale were donated to a foundation for the poor of Cortina. It was a sign of destiny, for the structure is a hospital today.

*these and following pages*
In the barroom at Valcastello can be found not only precious Venetian glasses, but also inventories of wines dating back from the 1920s onwards

NOBLE RUSSIAN VODKA

As for the castle, a few stones and ruined walls can still be seen, but everything else has vanished. Just like the countess's silverware, buried by her butler under the tallest of the pine trees before the arrival of the Austrians. The tons of Italian shells that fell on their position at Son Pauses over the following days changed the appearance of the mountains forever, burying the memory of the two "Englishwomen."

## THE LAST CASTLE: VALCASTELLO AT TOBLACH

In the absence of any documents or images that could be used to retrace life at the Castello di Sant'Uberto, we decided to photograph the very similar Valcastello, which lies a bit farther away, between Innichen and Toblach, or San Candido and Dobbiaco as they are known in Italian. It provides a unique testimony to the way of life of families and hunters at the beginning of the century, a golden age when it was common to have a glass of champagne on your return from a walk.

Here, too, everything turns around a passion for animals and the hunt.

The castle was constructed in the nineteenth century over the ruins of an older building, and is still the property of the family of the Counts of Acquarone, who had it rebuilt at the beginning of the twentieth century.

Pietro d'Acquarone (1890–1948), born into a noble family, was a minister to the Royal Household of Italy and an advisor to King Victor Emmanuel III of Savoy and Crown Prince Umberto. In 1943, he went down in history for the fundamental role he played in the fall of the Fascism regime mediating between the king and the fasist Grand Council in their plot to remove Mussolini.

Before the Second World War, Pietro had moved with his wife Maddalena Trezza di Musella and their four children to Valcastello, where he organized hunts which included the king. The grand royal hunts held in the 1930s in the presence of the princes of the House of Savoy have gone down in history.

On Pietro's death, the property was inherited by his son Cesare and his wife Claire Diericx. The couple brought Valcastello to life with their shared passion for hunting. A passion that would often take them to Africa. Many years after Charles Kenneth Howard-Bury's undertaking, the inhabitans of the Bengali village asked Claire to hunt a dangerous tiger that was attacking their children and terrorizing the village. The embalmed tiger is now in Valcastello.

Today their daughter Chantal d'Acquarone, an excellent rider and polo player and horse, lives in the castle with her husband and children.

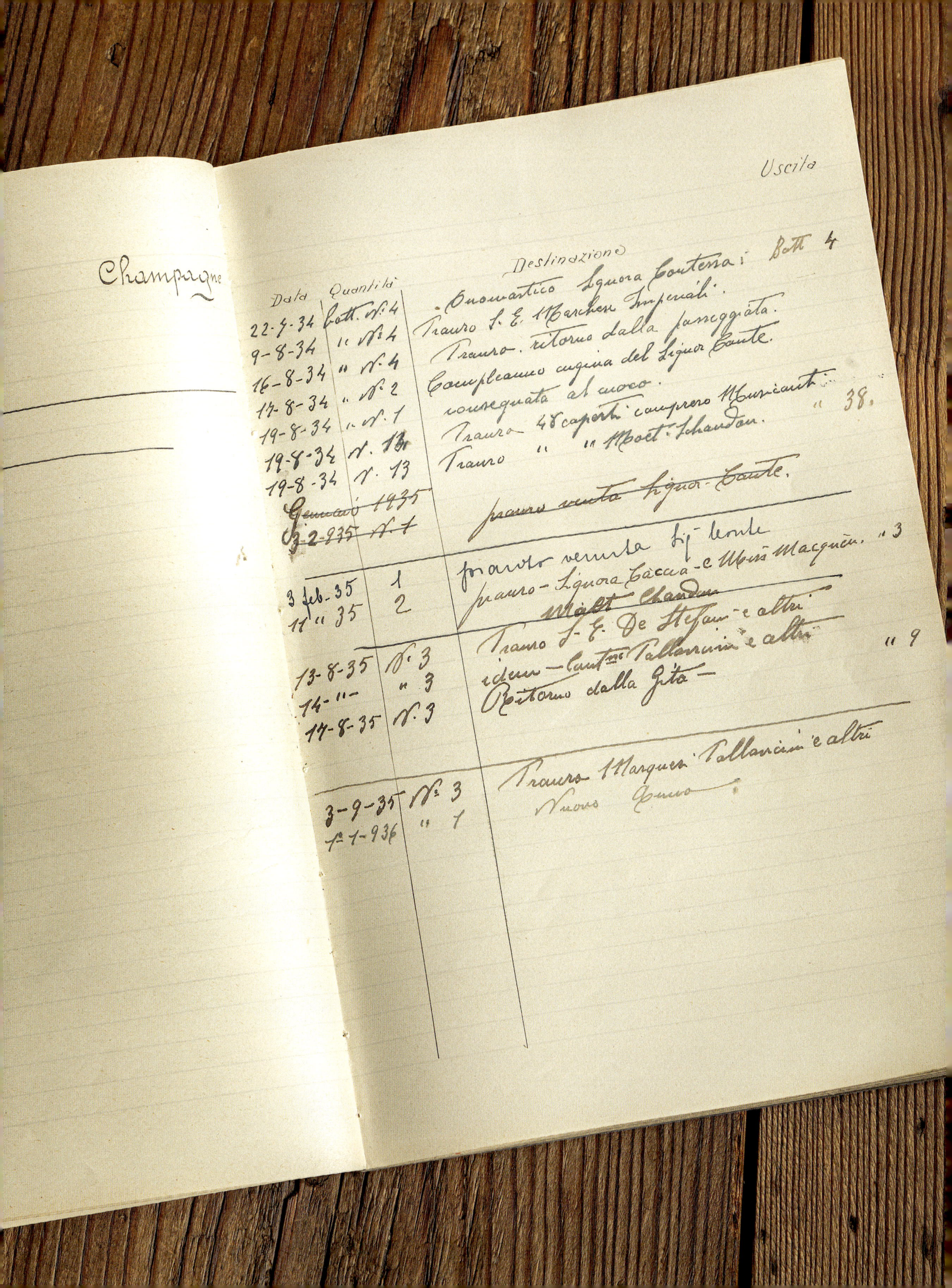

Uscita
Champagne
Data
Quantità
Destinazione
22-7-34 Bott. N. 4
9-8-34 " N. 4
16-8-34 " N. 4
17-8-34 " N. 2
19-8-34 " N. 1
Trauro. ritorno dalla passeggiata.
Compleanno cugina del Signor Conte.
consegnata al cuoco.
Moet Chandon
Gennaio 1935
3 feb-35 1
11 " 35 2
13-8-35 N. 3
14-8-35 N. 3
Ritorno dalla Gita
3-9-35 N. 3
1-1-936 " 1
Nuovo Anno

# SUMMER ANIMALS

## THE PECULIAR ORGANIZATION OF *LE REGOLE*

The relationship between people and animals in Cortina is so close that for centuries they used to live side by side in barns where the part devoted to the animals was considerably larger and better maintained than the one used by humans. Here, as in all mountain villages, livestock is a matter of survival. Sheep are fundamental for their wool and meat, and cows and horses are equally important. For instance, the alpine pastures known as *malghe* are used by herdsmen to milk their cows and make ricotta, butter, and cheese.

The pastoral tradition is still very much alive. Sheep are taken to high-altitude pastures at the end of spring and are brought back down from these Alps around October. It is a fine spectacle to see the sheep all following a single shepherd as he leads them to the place where the families that own them are waiting. They are able to recognize their animals by means of a tag on the ear called a *ra noda*. These ancient signs are handed down from father to son. When people have the same name, it is modified by a small addition, referring to a character trait or a nickname. The entire archive of symbols is listed in the *Book of Signs*.

The shepherd who in sole charge of the sheep is chosen each spring from among *regolieri* (lacal traditional families) and cannot turn the job down.

*left*
A table laid in the home of Alessia Bianchi Bormioli with ceramics decorated with a typical cow motif

*left*
A large ceramic cow decorates the table on the terraces of Franco Toffoletto and Maurizia Villa's home

*right*
Old milk churns made of tin line the bannister in Osanna Visconti's home

These ancient *regole* or rules, originally transmitted orally and then written down, are called the *laudi* and govern the management of the pastures. They are a democratic expression of the whole population with regard to the administration of their property.
The system is probably of Celtic origin since there is no trace of it in Roman law. Originally this set of *regole* was limited to the pastures, but it was then extended to cover the forest and eventually the whole of the Ampezzo valley. A common administration of property has been maintained in Cortina in spite of all the wars and the various transfers of control of the region between Austria and the Veneto.
In the sixteenth century, Rudolf II, Archduke of Austria and Holy Roman Emperor (1552–1612), confirmed the region's autonomous privileges, and this remained the situation for centuries. Cortina was free to govern its territory without interference. The Italian state has also passed specific laws to protect the distinctive character of Regole Ampezzane.
The members of the ancient order of the *regolieri* are still drawn today from the descendants of families originating from the Ampezzo valley. Its scope is to preserve collective respect for the territory, a harmony between humanity and nature. It is thanks to the *regole* that the population has been able to survive and grow affluent. In fact they govern 16,000 hectares of forest, since 1990 the Natural Park of the Dolomites, and above all the scale of the trade in timber.

*following pages*
A large cow embroidered on fabric in a corner of Simona Gandolfi and Hubertus von Hohenlohe's living room, surrounded by collages made by the master of the house

STREIF

Cortina

*previous pages*
Milking stools and cowbells are often used to decorate the interiors of houses, here in the homes of Alessia Bianchi Bormioli and the architects Stefano Gris and Silvia Dainese

*above*
At Valcastello Poloclub the home team trains for the annual polo tournament on snow in Cortina, held at Fiames. The horse is a recurrent feature of the interior decoration and furnishings in many of the valley's homes

*this page, right*
The stables at Valcastello; a horse's head carved in wood

*right*
An original console table in the form of a horse made by Hubert Le Gall in Casa Clerici

The stables at Valcastello

*following pages*
A bathroom at Valcastello decorated entirely on an equestrian theme

Among the animals of the summer most often represented in the mountains we find various kinds of bird, a theme often explored by interior designers: two excellent examples are, here below, a wooden bannister designed by Tito Lebreton for Nicola Giol's Ca' dei Fiori and, on the right, a table with feet in the shape of birds

*previous and these pages*
Table laid with Herrend china and ceramic decorations representing birds chosen by Nicola Giol for Ca' dei Fiori

Plaquettes inlaid in marble depicting various species of bird adorn a seventeenth-century escritoire of Venetian provenance

# SUMMER MATERIALS

Edoardo Gellner showed great mastery in mixing natural elements such as stone and wood with concrete, creating an immediately recognizable style

## THE STONE: DOLOMITE

In 1791, the French geologist, mineralogist, and vulcanologist Déodat de Dolomieu published in a physics journal the results of his research into a certain kind of rock he had found in the Italian Alps: "a type of limestone that effervesces very little with acids and is phosphorescent when struck." The samples analyzed in Geneva by the Swiss chemist Nicolas de Saussure confirmed the unique nature of this rock, which would be named after its discoverer.

So the rock dolomite, the mineral dolomite, and the mountain range of the Dolomites would all take their name from Dolomieu.

Before this, the range was generally known as the Monti Pallidi (Pale mountains) in reference to the particular whiteness of the rocks in this part of the Alps. The new name was popularized in the book *The Dolomite Mountains* by Gilbert and Churchill published in 1864 and then appeared on a map of the Austro-Hungarian Empire for the first time in 1876. It came into widespread use with the First World War.

The peculiarity of this rock is the presence of both calcium and magnesium carbonate. This unique composition is due to its geological origin and gives it a special beauty.

It took millions of years to form the ever-changing landscape of the Dolomites. The rock from which they are formed originated on the bottom of the tropical Tethys Sea. It is an accumulation of sediments and corals, covered with volcanic lava. As a result of the pressure exerted by the African tectonic plate against the Eurasian one, the Dolomites emerged from the water 135 million years ago. The plates are still converging today, causing the mountains to rise by 6 mm a year, despite their natural erosion.

Many relics of the time they spent under the water are still visible to

SEEKOFEL
CRISTALLO
SORAPIS
ANTELAO
FORMIN
NUVOLAU
NAVERAU
TOFANA

the naked eye on walks. Mollusks, sponges, skeletons of marine animals, corals and shells, ammonites, and the best known of all, the *pé de cioura* or "goat's foot," a *Megalodon* mollusk whose shape recalls the animal's footprint. They are believed to have given rise to the Ladin myth of the Anguane, water nymphs associated with rivers and lakes that are believed to be of great beauty despite their cloven feet.
A magnificent collection of over a thousand fossils can be seen in the Museo Paleontologico Rinaldo Zardini.
One of the peculiarities of the Cortina valley is that the rock descends all the way to the bottom, unlike other mountains that have grass or woods growing up on the heights.
The composition of the stone varies from peak to peak. On some mountains such as the Marmolada, Hohe Gaisl (Croda Rossa in Italian), or Monte Antelao limestone predominates, while others are the product of volcanic eruptions (the valley itself, for example) and the more recent such as Ra Stua, in the Alpe di Fosses, are made of marly material. The landscape of the Dolomites is, however, dominated by the presence of the friable dolomite rock which gave rise 223 million years ago to the massive structures of the Tre Cime di Lavaredo, Monte Cristallo, Pomagagnon, and part of the Tofane. They are truly impressive: from the Tofane massif, which exceeds 3,200 m (10,500 ft) in height, to the Marmolada, the highest of all at 3,342 m (10,968 ft), passing through those postcard favorites, the Tre Cime di Lavaredo. The range formed by these giants is unique and led in June 2009 to the declaration of the Dolomites as a UNESCO World Heritage Site.
The reflective properties caused by dolomite's distinctive composition of calcium and magnesium carbonate result in a spectacle known as alpenglow, or *enrosadira* in Italian. This is an optical phenomenon seen at sunrise and sunset which turns the mountains first red and then purple. The mountains appear to catch fire, which has given rise to many legends, including that of King Laurin, who had laid a curse on the Rosengarten group: no human eye would ever be able to admire it, neither by day nor by night. But the king had forgotten dawn and sunset. Since that time, at these two moments of the day, the mountains are tinged with pink.

An extremely rare late nineteenth-century wooden plate inlaid with the tarkashi technique represents the town of Cortina and the mountains with their original Austrian place names

# "ON MINERALOGICAL EXPEDITIONS IN THE MOUNTAINS OF TYROL WITH MONSIEUR FLEURIAU DE BELLEVUE, I FOUND A VAST AMOUNT OF CALCAREOUS ROCK"

Déodat de Dolomie, in *Journal de physique* (1791)

*above*
Entrance to the *stube* in the home designed by Edoardo Gellner for the Menardi family, now owned by Silvia Iliceto

*right*
The Dolomites tower above the town of Cortina in this picture by an Italian painter of the early twentieth century

## THE ARTISANS OF FIRE: BLACKSMITHS, MASTERS OF IRON, PEWTER, AND COPPER

The blacksmiths of Cortina were able to quickly make all the iron tools and accessories needed in people's daily lives: everything from horseshoes to cowbells.

The craft of metalworking in Cortina is not something taught at school but a tradition that has been handed down in family-run workshops. The raw material comes from the mines at Passo Giau or the nearby Castello di Andraz. In the nineteenth century there were seventy-seven workers of stone and metal in Cortina and old texts, such as a letter sent to the municipal authorities by Francesco Michieli in 1827, describe how the artisans of Cortina tried to get hold of steel, a metal essential to their trade.

The forging of metal has been practiced for centuries and has given rise to many surnames in the region: Fabbri, Fabbro, de Faveri, Favaro... The *fabbro* (blacksmith) plays an important role in the community. He is the one who has mastered fire, a prerogative attributed in ancient times to the gods, using procedures and methods that have not changed for hundreds of years. To enter a blacksmith's forge is to take a leap back in time: the rhythmic sound of the hammer striking the anvil, the smell of burning coal... Generations have learned the trade by imitating master craftspeople, and elevated the working of wrought iron into an art, molding and shaping the metal.

A family of ironworkers that has been living in Cortina since the fourteenth century has its coat of arms on the old town hall, and thanks to both an important donation to the Museo delle Regole and Paolo Giacomel's book *La fucina artistica dei "Càiser"* we are able to grasp the extent of their talent. Francesco Demenego-Caiser learned the craft of making keys and locks in Vienna and handed it down to his grandsons Modesto (1896–1982) and Ugo (1900–1991), who would take their expertise as far as the Egyptian court. Their MUD hallmark can be found on a number of objects from the former royal palace in Cairo.

This long tradition of transmission from father to son continues in Cortina today, in new locations such as Pian da Lago for Candeago, or in Fiammes for the brothers Marco and Renzo Zardini.

*right*
A door made of wood and wrought iron, a typical example of the skill of Ampezzo's artisans

*top*
A folksy tin bath tub at Osanna Visconti's

*right*
An old safe set in a wooden wall
in Paola Caovilla's home

*following pages*
Gris Dainese architects have reinterpreted iron in a modern key in the interiors of a contemporary barn designed for the Santel family at Gilardon. The blued steel mesh protects the black faux-cement staircase, surrounded by modern paneling of grayed spruce

## OTHER, MORE OR LESS PRECIOUS METALS

Iron is not the only metal worked by artisans. There are others, too, such as copper, brass, silver, and tin.

Pewter is a particular favorite in mountain villages. Once one of the materials most widely used for everyday objects in Cortina, pewter is an alloy composed mainly of tin, to which small amounts of copper and antimony are added. It has many advantages: it does not oxidize, is not hazardous to health, it lasts for generations, and has an attractive, shiny color. It had pride of place in any house in the valley.

While pewter has been worked since ancient times, it was not until the sixteenth century that it came into widespread use in Europe. At first the objects made from pewter were fairly simple, but then grew more complex thanks to the dexterity of Venetian and Bohemian artisans, who developed the ability to produce articles of great value. Fascinating examples often to be found in the antique stores of Cortina are the *brocche di corporazione*, large vessels with a highly decorated octagonal base that were used at meetings of artisans and guilds on feast days. They have a variety of forms, depending on their origin: beaked, pot-bellied, narrow...

Pewter is said to be the fourth most precious metal, after platinum, gold, and silver. However, the rapid spread of earthenware and china in the nineteenth century led to a reduction in the use of objects made from pewter in the home, although they can still be found in the abundant collections of the families of the valley.

*previous pages*
The artist Alice Mocellin has created an oxidized iron sculpture with the title *Bosco* (*Forest*) for a wall in her home

*right*
A table laid with pewter dishes that bear witness to a great tradition of the Ampezzo valley in Casa Visconti

*following pages*
A vast collection of pewter objects adorns various rooms in Casa Alverà

IHS

*previous pages*
In the kitchen of Alice Mocellin's home a collection of aluminum cheese molds and, right, a plate rack with various metal and ceramic articles in a small house at Chiave

In the Ampezzo valley brass is often used to decorate rooms as well. Right, a collection of embossed brass plates at Ca' Alleluia

This kitchen, made all the warmer thanks to the use of copper, was designed by the architect Roberto Gerosa, responsible for the restoration of Casa Alverà

*following pages*
Bronze brightens up Osanna Visconti's creations in the home of Alessia Bianchi Bormioli. The copper washbasin in a bathroom of the same house

Khaled Hosseini
Il cacciatore di aquiloni
PIEMME
ROMANA PETRI OVUNQUE IO SIA
VENEZIA CADUTA E SALVEZZA
SANSONI
il libro della MANO
Goldschmiedt
Alfieri & Lacroix Editore

# MOVIES AND WRITERS

## A REFUGE OF INTELLECTUALS

The relationship between Italian writers and Cortina got off to an unusual start around the large table and cooking range of a little-known figure, Rachele Padovan (1916–1999). Rachele was a farmer's daughter from Cortina who became a key figure in the cultural life of Cortina through her meeting with the writer Giovanni Comisso (1875–1965), who fell madly in love with her and would turn her refusal to marry him into a novel, *Un inganno d'amore* (Milan, 1942).
Thanks to her intelligence and fine cooking, she was able to turn her home into a coterie of writers, artists, and intellectuals of every kind, seating at her table people like Goffredo Parise, Andrea Zanzotto, Filippo de Pisis...
More reclusive, but just as passionate about Cortina, were the writers Dino Buzzati and Indro Montanelli.

*left*
One of the bedrooms at La Montanella, given this name because it was the residence of Indro Montanelli and Colette Rosselli. The house was designed by Luigi Vietti, but Colette chose the furnishings herself. The new owner has left the place almost exactly as it was

*right*
Giovanni Comisso in 1942

## INDRO MONTANELLI'S WALK

Indro Montanelli (1909–2001) was a frequent visitor to Cortina from the 1960s onward, mainly in summer and sometimes out of season, going there with the hope of recovering from his bouts of depression. Neither a great skier nor a climber, he commenced his methodical days with a pleasant walk along a route that would take his name after his death. The Montanelli Trail starts from Piè Tofana chalet and continues along a gentle slope through the pine trees as far as the Lago Ghedina crossroads.

In the collection of his letters published by Rizzoli he would say: "Every evening I watch with envy the climbers returning from their adventures on the rocks, far less tired than me. While they conquered the bracing crags, I have had to clamber along the far more arduous peaks of Idealism, Spiritualism, Calvinism and I can't tell you what other weird notions" (Indro Montanelli, *Nella mia lunga e tormentata esistenza: Lettere di una vita*, Milan, 2012.)

He married his third wife, the painter and illustrator Colette Rosselli, in Cortina on September 9, 1974, carving their first names and the date of their wedding into the coffee table of their home overlooking the Tofana.

*above*
Indro Montanelli at his summer residence in Cortina

*right*
On the desk, personal items belonging to Indro Montanelli and a book dedicated to him

A Indro,
collega in storia
e in giornalismo,
queste pagine
su un mondo
anche a lui caro,
col fraterno

*previous pages and left*
The large living room facing onto the valley with the wooden table on which the date of Indro and Colette's wedding is carved

*bottom*
A bedroom at La Montanella

While the movies shot in winter were mainly comedies, the ones set in summer are very different and far more dramatic. The mountains in summer are no laughing matter.

Climbing is a dangerous sport, and even love stories take on a poignant tone.

The earliest of these movies dates from 1919. It is a silent film directed by Erich von Stroheim, *Blind Husbands*. Among the opening titles is a geographic note: "Cortina d'Ampezzo, on the Austro-Italian border, the Mecca of American tourists," even though Cortina had become Italian on May 28, 1915, American tourism was still far off and the movie was actually shot in the United States...

This romantic drama about an Austrian officer and a young wife neglected by her husband, an American doctor, which reaches its climax on the slopes of Monte Cristallo, is a tribute to a young mountaineer, Sepp Innerkofler, who died on the mountain during the First World War.

The German genre of movies set in the mountains, known as *Bergfilme*, reached its height in the work of Arnold Franck and his protégé Luis Trenker (1892–1990), an architect and mountain guide as well as actor and producer. His films tirelessly promoted the uncompromising values of the mountains: *Berg des Schicksals* (*Mountain of Destiny*), 1924; *Berge in Flammen* (*Mountains on Fire*), 1931; and the West German–Italian coproduction *Flucht in die Dolomiten* or *Il prigioniero della montagna* (*Escape to the Dolomites*), 1955.

The fashion for movies of this kind would fade after the Second World War, and was not revived until 1993, when in Renny Harlin's film *Cliffhanger* Sylvester Stallone starred as a member of a mountain rescue team, defying vertigo on the faces of Lagazuoi, Cadini di Misurina, and the Cinque Torri.

The drama of the summer persists in the story of a tormented love affair in the 1968 film *Amanti* (*A Place for Lovers*). In this film Faye Dunaway and Marcello Mastroianni succumb to passion both on and off screen. Enrico Lucherini, the movie's press officer, has this to say

about the Italian actor: "He was crazy about her, but so jealous that he kept her locked up in the hotel all day" (Ludovica Damiani, *Set in Cortina*, 2010.)
The director Vittorio De Sica decided to shoot the film at one of the three mountain huts (*malghe*) in Fedarola, located on the road leading to the Dibona refuge. While the huts can still be seen today, the same cannot be said of the interiors, whose décor perfectly reflected the taste of the 1960s, as they were constructed in the studio.
Summer was to provide the inspiration for many other films in Cortina, including some that starred animals rather than humans: *Zanna Bianca alla riscossa* (*White Fang to the Rescue*) in 1974; *Ladyhawke* in 1985; and Jean-Jacques Annaud's *The Bear* in 1988, winner of numerous awards. The director was delighted with his choice of location: "The Alps offer a whole range of different, magnificent landscapes, easily accessible by myriad mountain roads and trails" (Ludovica Damiani, *Set in Cortina*, 2010.)

*left*
Marcello Mastroianni and Faye Dunaway in *Amanti* (*A Place for Lovers*, 1968); Sylvester Stallone in *Cliffhanger* (1993)

*top*
One of the small houses in the locality of Fedarola where Vittorio De Sica's film *Amanti* was shot (1968)

# SUMMER STYLE

## AUSTRIAN INFLUENCES AND THE COSTUMES OF AMPEZZO

Geographically situated on the border between the Republic of Venice and the Austrian Empire, to which it belonged for over four hundred years from 1511 until the end of the First World War, Cortina d'Ampezzo has remained faithful to the customs of the neighboring Ladin valleys and the Tyrol region. They shared a common history for centuries, in spite of the fact that Cortina d'Ampezzo benefited from a degree of autonomy that was renewed by each emperor.
While the Ladin language, derived in part from the ancient Celtic tongue (which is where place names like Crignes or Cianderies come from), is still alive, it is in women's dress that this Ladin influence is most evident. The traditional costumes of Ampezzo are very different from the Austrian-style dirndl worn by many summer visitors to Cortina, and are always donned by women on religious feast days or at events such as weddings or baptisms.
The typical Cortina costume was already drawing great admiration from visitors at the end of the eighteenth century. And in 1864 it was described by the writer and artist Josiah Gilbert in his book *The Dolomite Mountains*.
"The women, as they should be, were the prettiest sight of all [...]. Large aprons of a deep blue, over a black dress, edged with red; white sleeves, red stockings, a bright handkerchief of a well chosen tint, put like a ruff round the neck, a sprinkling of lace and ornaments, and the little black hat at top of all [...]" (Josiah Gilbert and George Cheetham Churchill, *The Dolomite Mountains*, 1864).
Particular types of costume are worn at different times of year and on different occasions. The *ra jàida* is for the winter season, consisting of a sober black Korean-style jacket fastened with nine cloth buttons and a striped apron.

*left*
A flowery corner at Valcastello. The *trompe-l'œil* wall was painted by Chantal d'Acquarone

*bottom*
Period photo of children in Tyrolean costume, 1920s/'30s. Marini archive

In summer women wear the *ra varnaza*, light everyday clothing. This costume is composed of a black shirt dress (*ciamesoto*) covered with a fringed scarf fastened by a filigree brooch (*pontapeto*) and an apron of shiny silk or wool (*palegrèn*). Under the *ciamesoto*, there is a white chemise with lace sleeves fastened with colored ribbons above the elbow. This is probably the costume that was described by Gilbert in 1864.
The third costume, the *ra magnes*, is the outfit worn at festivals. It is the most important, used on special occasions by all women, whether married or not, with the only thing distinguishing them being the wearing of a tulle scarf around the neck, the *drapo de racordela infizada*. This festive costume is strictly black, with a short jacket fastened only at the waist. The traditional black hat was embellished in the eighteenth century with ostrich feathers, probably borrowed from fashionable wear of tourists passing through the valley.
In the seventeenth century, there was another, more demure costume called the *ra vecia*, in which the breasts were covered by a stiff triangular piece of hand-embroidered cloth called the *pèza da sén*.
All three costumes are completed by the traditional low-set bun, gold drop-shaped earrings and essential filigree jewelry.

*bottom*
Village women in traditional dress, 1920s/'30s. Zeno archive

*right*
A traditional Austrian dirndl in Alessia Bianchi Bormioli's home

*following page, left*
A consolle table houses a small collection of Austrian drinking glasses at Ca' del Rite

*following page, right*
A corner decorated in typical Austrian style in Casa Gazzoni

*previous page, left*
Caterina Zangrando is a creative person: she makes jewelry and has a passion for embroidery

*previous page, right*
A summer dirndl belonging to Giovanna Giol

*above*
Cover of *En Tyrol* by Maurice Grandjean, 1893

*right*
A beautiful piece of embroidery in the Ampezzo style by Caterina Zangrando

# FILIGREE

The art of filigree has remote origins, documented as a way of working and binding gold and silver in Ur (the ancient capital of Sumeria) as early as 2500 BCE.
Its name in English comes from the Italian *filigrana*, which in turn derives from the union of two Latin words, *filum* meaning thread and *granum*, grain, and in this sense a small bead.
Filigree is a form of metalwork that consists in twisting, bending, and then soldering very fine metal threads (generally silver or pure gold) to form designs.
Filigree first appeared in Cortina in the seveneenth century. The technique came from Venice, where the goldsmith's art was highly advanced, and certain craftsmen specialized in it. Handed down from father to son, the craft quickly developed into a production of very high quality. Such was the mastery of the of Ampezzo artisans that people would come to speak of the "Secret of Cortina" in relation to their invisible soldering technique and the extreme fineness of the pure silver threads.
The filigree jewelry produced in Cortina soon surpassed that of Venice and it became necessary to find a way to pass on this expertise. In 1846, a School of Design was set up to foster local artisans and encourage the people of Cortina in their natural bent for technical and artistic work. In 1856, this was renamed Scuola Industriale and placed under the direction of Gian Maria Ghedini, trained at the Accademia delle Belle Arti in Venice, who introduced courses in the arts of cabinetmaking, mosaic and filigree.
In 1874, the institution was turned into a state–run school, subsidized by the Austrian Ministry of Commerce, and SFC (Scuola Filigrana Cortina) became one of the most sought-after hallmarks. Many of its students opened their own filigree workshops upon leaving school in order to meet the rising demand from tourists.
The Permanent Exhibition staged on the ground floor of the school allowed visitors to the town with a taste for jewelry and objets d'art in general to satisfy their desire for souvenirs.
The First World War and the subsequent transfer of Ampezzo to Italy led to an abrupt halt to the production of filigree, which gradually began to die out. It was a single family, the Verocai, who saved the craft from total extinction. Items from the school have become much sought-after museum pieces, and women will often wear reproductions of the jewelry over their traditional costumes out of fear of losing the precious originals.

In Cortina filigree was utilized both for refined hair ornaments and for more traditional jewelry such as brooches, necklaces, and pendants in the shape of a cross. There were specific rules governing the location and form of the ornaments for the hair: below a heavy bun plaited at the nape of the neck, two fine hairpins ending in pommels of identical structure but different sizes; on the right of the bun were fixed the magnificent and very light filigree flowers called *trèmui*, inspired by local flora, in particular edelweiss, gentians, and daisies. The flowers were also used to indicate a woman's marital status: single women were only allowed one, while married women could wear as many as they wished. It is the way the flowers tremble on the spring with every movement of the head that gives them the name *trèmui*.

*right*
Filigree *bujele* (hatpins) from the late nineteenth century

*following pages*
Various examples of the art of filigree "de Anpezo"; left the *trèmui* are contained in a Bohemian pocket drinking cup from the Biedermeier period

The inhabitants of the valley also produced their own textiles. From a very early date, they grew flax and hemp, making them independent in the manufacture of their clothing, household linen, or fabrics for everyday use.

The seeds were sown in spring and the plants harvested at the end of August. The stalks were then spread out to ret until late fall, when they were gathered into sheaves called *mannelli*. Each small village used to be equipped with a communal oven in which the *mannelli* were dried to get rid of superfluous material, or the women would simply warm up the sheaves of linen or hemp by wearing them. A final cleaning at home, and then came the spinning, which took long hours of work. Although there were professional weavers, each house still had its own loom. Women took full responsibility for making linen from the flax. They were the ones who "sowed the seeds, harvested the plants, retted and dried the flax, carded it, and finally spun it. And who knew how to embroider the traditional fabrics."

A whole year would pass between sowing and weaving, which explains why this activity was soon abandoned, even though many nostalgic descriptions of the flax fields of Cortina dotted with blue flowers have come down to us.

Sheep's wool was another source of cloth used for a variety of purposes. The whitest yarn was made into lace and used to adorn household linen and traditional blouses.

*Lana cotta*, or boiled wool, is one of the oldest fabrics, and has been used by Tyrolean shepherds since the twelfth century for its waterproof properties and unique warmth.

The name of the most iconic of these materials, loden, comes from the word *lodo*, or ball of wool. The yarn was spun and woven by the peasants of the Dolomites to be used as protection (cloaks, boots, hats) against bad weather, and had the same gray color as raw sheep's wool. After being endorsed by the emperor Franz Joseph, who wore it while hunting, it gained respectability among the upper classes and grew more sophisticated. Made out of finer merino wool, its color was changed from white to red and then to the famous shade of green with which it has been identified ever since.

While weaving was mainly carried out in the home, there are records of families who specialized in the craft in the Bruneck region. In 1776, a certain Josef Franz, originally from Bohemia, opened a textile mill. The shift from the dobby loom to the more modern Jacquard loom would allow the emergence of new types of fabric and patterns.

Little by little, the classic Tyrolean fabrics with distinctive Alpine designs began to appear. They were used not only for traditional costumes but also for sheets, curtains, bedspreads, and tablecloths. Decorated with motifs of edelweiss, stags, and hearts, they are clearly visible in an archive photo from 1910 of the window of the Cooperativa, which soon came to sell them by the meter.

*right*
The old *stua* in Casa Rosa Menardi at Gilardon with the traditional household linen. This is a very old house bearing the date 1746 on the ridgepole of the roof

## THE COOPERATIVA

*top*
The Cooperativa in Cortina in 1910. Archivio fotografico La Cooperativa di Cortina

*bottom*
Typical fabrics from the Cooperativa possessed by every family in Cortina

Cortina's Cooperativa was set up at the Bozen Chamber of Commerce in 1893 and was the first consumer cooperative in South Tyrol. Located in an old grain store, it offers basic commodities at moderate prices. In economic terms, it served to exercise a degree of price control and its social function was to provide its members with hard-to-obtain goods and other benefits.

It is interesting to note that as early as 1893 fabrics were among the goods sold by the cooperative, alongside flour and maize. In 1938, the store was divided into three departments of equal importance: food, textiles, and hardware.

Moving from basic premises at Pontechiesa to its new location on Corso Italia, the store now has a floor space of over 4,000 square meters, and continues to promote local crafts and is one of the key centers of life in Cortina.

*right*
Lace and embroidery on white linen were a tradition of the women of Ampezzo and can still be found in many bedrooms, here in Nicola Giol's Ca' dei Fiori

*following pages*
In the same home, decorated by Tito Lebreton, two bedrooms perfectly reflect the way Cortina is poised between Tyrol and the Veneto

## A BOHEMIAN WIND BLOWS IN THE 1950S AND 1960S: LADY CORTINA AND THE *SIGNORA DI CORTINA*

Two women would leave their mark on the festive Cortina of the 1950s and '60s with their beauty, their energy, typical of the time, their love affairs, and their parties and art of hospitality.

Lady Europa was the title won by Ira von Fürstenberg in a Europe-wide beauty contest held in Cortina in 1965. Ira was at home in the valley, having spent many vacations at the magnificent chalet called Villa Bella owned by her mother Clara Agnelli and her second husband, Giovanni Nuvoletti. Contemporary photos show her growing up, from bridesmaid at the wedding of Maximilian zu Windisch-Graetz in 1946 to a (very) young bride herself and then the mother of two children winning the title of the most beautiful woman in Europe.

Bohemia was in Ira's blood—she was one third Hungarian, one third Italian, and one third Austrian—and defined her temperament. It was during a winter spent in Cortina in 1959 that she tried to save her marriage to Alfonso von Hohenlohe (married in 1955 and divorced in 1960), and it was there that she taught her two sons to ski, a sport that would become a passion for the younger of them. And it was there that a paparazzo caught her dancing cheek-to-cheek with the international playboy Baby Pignatari.

Many families of the Austrian nobility, such as the Fürstenbergs, Hohenlohes, and Windisch-Graetzs, used to frequent Cortina in the period immediately after the war. This aristocratic society would gradually be infiltrated by wealthy members of a flourishing Italian entrepreneurial bourgeoisie. As Marina Cicogna put it, "the town started to open up to tourism on the part of great families and industrial groups." These included members of the Agnelli, Barilla, Zanussi, Mondadori, and Marzotto families. It was from this latter family of industrialists from Vicenza that the woman who would earn the nickname of the Signora di Cortina came: Marta Marzotto.

The model Marta Vacondio married Umberto Marzotto on December 18, 1954, and was introduced by him to the Dolomites, a place to which she would remain attached for the rest of her life, spending long months there both in summer and in winter, from December to March, with the highlights of New Year's Eve and the celebration of her birthday on February 24.

Marta quickly became the undisputed

*below*

An unusual outfit for Ira von Fürsteberg: she is dressed as a waitress during a famous soirée at Casa Vietti in the 1960s. Franchetti archive

A smiling Marta Marzotto in a photo from the early 1960s. Franchetti archive

*right*

One of Marta Marzotto's dirndls which she gave to Chiara Reale

queen of all parties, dinners, and social events. In the winter of 1954, Marina Cicogna wrote: "We went with the flow and the flow could not fail to bring to our home Marta Marzotto, who at the time was the beating heart of high society in Cortina."

It was at her kitchen table that the cult film *Anonimo veneziano* (released in English as *The Anonymous Venetian*) was born. Marta relates in her biography how Giuseppe Berto and Enrico Maria Salerno "worked on the screenplay surrounded by trays of *puccia* and various kinds of salami and cheese" (Marta Marzotto, *Smeraldi a colazione*, 2016).

In another legendary film shot in the Dolomites, *Dance of the Vampires*, its stars Sharon Tate and Roman Polanski are seen dancing at Marta's place on New Year's Eve in 1967: "Sharon with a wreath of flowers in her hair and a very light blouse of white silk looked like the queen of hippies."

Her house was so full of children and friends that she put the sign "Kinderheim Marzotto" up on its door. This was in the May of 1968, during the hippie years, and Marta's colorful style was inspired by local folklore. With her friend Vittoria Cappelli, she opened Turlututù, a store located close to the Hotel de la Poste. The boutique sold everything from rugs to custom jewelry, and above all clothing in a folk style made up of bright colors and fringes that she applied to coats, boots, and even gloves. Many wardrobes in Cortina bear traces of her colorful creations, like the beloved dirndls she gave to her daughters, nieces, and friends.

Cortina was one of her favorite places. In an article entitled "Dolce vita sulle nevi," published in *la Repubblica*, she confided to the journalist Laura Laurenzi: "I miss my fireplace, my red and green loden couches, my ever so special sitting room and always magical Cortina." While it was Luigi Vietti who designed the fireplace of her home and the antique dealer Claudio Zanettin who helped her put together her multiple collections, a jumble of old bars of soap, sacred objects, and all kinds of trimmings, it was from Marta and her alone that came her innate sense of decoration and art of mixing styles; an admixture that she would also apply to her relations with people throughout her life. With a fantastic ability in public relations and being such a wonderful hostess, she turned her salon into a haunt of the intelligentsia and through her the rather closed society of postwar Cortina was invaded by actors, writers, directors, sports stars and politicians.

In the book she wrote about Cortina in the 1960s, Marina Cicogna concluded that it was "a social life that never made the great leap to an international level like St. Moritz or Gstaad but remained very Italian." It is this Italian air that can still be breathed today, and that makes Cortina so special and lovable. In addition to the people of the Ampezzo valley, its inhabitants and visitors come from all the major cities of Italy: Rome above all, but also Milan, Bologna, Florence, Naples, Genoa, and its neighbors Venice, Verona, Padua, and Treviso. Which explains the eclecticism of the town's interiors.

*left*
A close-up of the table setting in Marta Marzotto's home

*above*
Marta Marzotto at a party in the 1960s. Franchetti archive

*following pages*
Marta Marzotto's dining room has hosted many personalities from the worlds of culture, politics, and art as well as members of the international jet set

FOLK STYLE

The eclectic style that characterizes Cortina's homes also harks back to floral decorations and folkly motifs. The Zangrando home contains a bedspread embroidered with the owners' personal motif; the Gazzoni kitchen has a collection of folksy fabrics used as curtains to cover the utensils cupboards in the stone walls.

The doors of a built-in wardrobe decorated with figures in costume painted in a popular style by an artist in the family brighten up a room in a house in Cortina

*following pages*
Fabrics in a folk style warm up corners of the *stube* in Alessia Bianchi Bormioli's home

ARTOIS
AUVERGNE
POITOU
ALSACE
GUYENNE
BERRY
GUYENNE
GUYENNE

*left*
A fabric with a floral pattern covers
the walls of Casa Gazzoni

*top*
A motif of roses painted on wood adorns
a wall in Casa Clavarino

Cortina specialized in woodcarving, and the surrounding valleys, including Val di Fassa, in the typically Tyrolean art of painting wooden furniture. Painting was an easy way of covering up flaws in simpler types of wood like deal, and softwood in general. It was an activity that could be carried out all year round and on a multitude of objects in addition to furniture, from store signs and door panels to sleds. The motifs characteristic of the Val di Fassa were birds and the most widely used color was blue. Thanks to its itinerant painters, Val di Fassa would leave its mark on the design of rural furniture throughout the Puster valley and neighboring regions, including Cortina.

Right up to the eighteenth and nineteenth centuries, the colors of the Baroque style found their way onto furniture.

The motifs were mainly flowers such as tulips and carnations in vases or bouquets, along with animals. Birds were represented alone or in pairs as a symbol of love, or simply shown roosting in the Tree of Life. Painters would also simulate marble or wood grain.

A closet and chest of drawers made of painted wood in Casa Gazzoni

*following pages*
Other examples of decoration on wood, the jamb of a door in Casa Alverà and a wardrobe in Casa Zangrando

## RELIGIOSITY

Religion has deep roots in Cortina d'Ampezzo. The earliest document mentioning the presence of a church in Ampezzo dates from 1203. Each little village had its own church, referred to indiscriminately as a *chiesa*, a *chiesetta*, or a *cappella*.

In addition to the basilica, there are eighteen places of worship still in use today, run by the members of their founding confraternities. The most important of these religious buildings is the basilica of Santi Filippo e Giacomo, built between 1769 and 1775 and famous for its campanile, which has become the symbol of Cortina. Constructed of white dolomite stone and renovated from 1852 to 1858 by Silvestro Franceschi, who replaced the decaying old structure with one designed by the Viennese engineer Hermann Bergmann, the tower has given life in Ampezzo its rhythm. Its great bells were saved from destruction by Charles I, Emperor of Austria. Enchanted by their sound, he decided not to have them melted down in spite the need to supply lead for artillery during the First World War. There are six main bells and three special ones: the Campana dell'Agonia for funerals, the Campana dell'Orologio, and the Campana del Guardafuoco, used until 1910 as a fire alarm.

In the old days in the Ampezzo Valley a crucifix used to be placed between houses, and small places of worship were built along country lanes and at crossroads. In popular belief, they offered protection against evil spirits and supernatural powers. What made Cortina different from other settlements in the valley is that these chapels were soon replaced by churches, whence their abundance.

The religiosity of the people of Ampezzo still finds concrete expression in the habit of prayer, regular church attendance, and a multitude of festivals. One of the most important is held on August 14, the night before the Feast of the Assumption, when huge bonfires are lit throughout the valley to celebrate the cutting of hay. Another mode of expression is in processions, such as that of the Madonna della Difesa, held on January 19 to celebrate Mary's miraculous intervention in defense of the people of Ampezzo in 572, or those of the Santissimo Rosario and Corpus Domini.

*right*
In Marta Marzotto's home a collection of religious images of various periods and origins

*following page, left*
Statues representing various figures, typical of Neapolitan nativity scenes, in Osanna Visconti's bedroom

*following page, right*
A wooden niche in Paola Caovilla's home displaying nativity statues

*previous page, left*
In the master bedroom of Ca' Alleluia, a collection of holy pictures and ex-votos

*previous page, right*
A collection of large wooden rosaries hangs on the wall of a bedroom in Simona Gandolfi and Hubertus von Hohenlohe's home

Right, corners of Casa Alverà with a large collection of images of the Virgin Mary; above, a statue of St. George slaying the dragon

A pictorial testimony to the long tradition of rustic wooden capitals that were used to mark crossroads

# SUMMER FLAVORS

## "PAN E POLENTA FAN FAMIGLIA CONTENTA" ("BREAD AND POLENTA MAKE FOR A HAPPY FAMILY")

The cuisine of the Ampezzo valley is the product of tradition and the seasons. It is *cucina povera*, a simple, humble fare made from the ingredients offered by the land or grown locally. Every family cultivated its own *orto*, or vegetable garden, making it independent from the community and ensuring that its members were never in danger of going hungry.

Feeding the family, like tending the kitchen garden or caring for the domestic animals that were an essential part of people's diet, has always been women's work. They would milk the cows in the morning and then use the milk to make a wide variety of products. Cheese, fresh or smoked ricotta, butter, and cream were strictly homemade up until the beginning of the last century. The tradition is maintained even today on the *malghe*. Another very useful animal was the pig, whose meat would be turned into what has become a local specialty, a smoked ham called speck.

Women were also responsible for making bread, including the traditional *puccia*, which can be thin and crunchy or soft with cumin and fennel seeds, an essential accompaniment to cold meats and local cheeses. In the mountains, bread was also used in rituals: it was given to newlyweds and mothers who had just given birth, and was offered at funerals (*pan da morto* with anise seeds).

Favorites in the *orto* were beetroot and cabbage, easy to preserve for the winter in the form of *crauti*, or sauerkraut. The potato, a staple food, reigned supreme: cooked, boiled, or fried, it was used in a vast range of dishes. And then there were onions, garlic, *cren* (horseradish), and poppy, whose seeds added a final touch to many recipes.

At the end of summer, people turned to the woods, abounding in wild fruit like strawberries, bilberries, and cowberries. Often collected by children in large baskets, the fruit would be turned into jam and used to make desserts. Pinecones were collected for their pine nuts; elderflowers and rosehips were used to flavor syrups and grappa.

Surprisingly, mushroom picking was not widespread before the First World War, as most varieties, apart from chanterelles, were avoided on suspicion of being poisonous.

Desserts are seasonal too: the raspberries of summer are used to produce delicious specialty tarts by the Lovat and Embassy *pasticcerie*, as well as a hot syrup that is poured over ice cream at high-altitude refuges or lakeside chalets.

*left*
A picnic basket from the 1950s preserved at Valcastello

## LINZER TORTE



- *250 gr flour*
- *250 gr hazelnut flour*
- *250 gr sugar*
- *250 gr butter*
- *2 eggs plus one yolk*
- *raspberry jam*
- *a pinch of salt*
- *a teaspoon of cinnamon*
- *a generous pinch of ground cloves*
- *lemon zest*

*Sieve the flour onto the countertop with the hazelnut flour and make a well in the center. Put the sugar, spices, and the two eggs in the well, around the butter cut into pieces. Blend rapidly until the mixture is smooth and then place it in the fridge for an hour. Roll out two-thirds of the pastry and use it to line a shallow cake tin. Spread with raspberry jam and cover with a lattice made from strips of the remaining pastry. Brush with a beaten egg yolk. Bake at 180°C for around 45 minutes.*

*left*
A set of original Venetian glasses with a floral decoration from the 1910s in Casa Zangrando

*this page*
A door decorated with painted flowers and fruit in Alice Mocellin's home

## SKIWASSER

*Summer version of "ski water," served in Alpine refuges as a refreshing and fortifying drink for climbers and trekkers.*

- *2 spoonfuls of raspberry syrup*
- *2 spoonfuls of lemon juice*
- *250 ml sparkling water (or tonic)*

*Pour all the ingredients into a glass, mix well, and serve chilled with ice.*

The furniture in the dining room of this house was painted in a folk style by the owner's aunt, an artist

*following page, left*
An antique wooden rack for loaves of *puccia* decorates the dining room of an old, completely renovated barn

*following page, right*
A view of the living area in Casa Gris Dainese. The table is custom-built from oak and the paneling is made of salvaged deal, as is the floor which comes from a barn

## SPECK

- *leg of pork*
- *crushed coarse salt*
- *black pepper in grains*
- *cloves*
- *bay leaves, to taste*
- *garlic*
- *saltpeter, as required*

*Choose the best-quality lean leg of pork, deboned, salted and seasoned.*
*The curing is done in tubs for 2–3 weeks, depending on the size of the leg, and the meat must be basted every day with its own brine.*
*The smoking is done with a choice variety of wood and juniper berries. The speck should then be dried, kept in a cool place, and consumed after 5 or 6 months.*

*Recipe taken from Francesca Gaspari and Maria Luisa Menardi,* Coŝlùpe frìte e lòchi 'n técia: Raccolta di ricette della tradizione ampezzana *(Cortina d'Ampezzo: no date).*

*right*
Salami, speck, and würstel accompanied by mini pretzels are always to be found on the table in Anna Marzotto's home

# BIBLIOGRAPHY


Alverà, Pietro. *Cronaca di Ampezzo nel Tirolo dagli antichi tempi fino al ventesimo secolo*. Edited by Carlo Gandini. Cortina d'Ampezzo, 2002.

Arnoldo, Morena. *Da un filo d'argento... L'arte della filigrana in Ampezzo: Storia di una tradizione*. Cortina d'Ampezzo, 2003.

Baker, Carlos, *Ernest Hemingway: A Life Story*. New York, 1969.

Baker, Carlos, ed. *Ernest Hemingway: Selected Letters, 1917–1961*. New York, 1981.

Ball, John. *Peaks, Passes, and Glaciers: A Series of Excursions by Members of the Alpine Club* (1859). Norderstedt, 2020.

Ballario, Piera. *Fiabe e leggende delle Dolomiti*. Florence, 1993.

Belli, Mario Ferruccio. *Storia di Cortina d'Ampezzo 1914–1918*. Maniago, 2014.

Boschian, Nada. *Il peltro*. Milan, 1996.

Cenacchi, Giovanni. *Gli Scoiattoli di Cortina: Storia e memoria di 50 anni d'alpinismo ampezzano*. Cortina d'Ampezzo, 1989.

Chilton, Meredith, and Claudia Lehener-Jobst. *Fired by Passion: Vienna Baroque Porcelain of Claudius Innocentius du Paquier*, 3 vols. Stuttgart, 2009.

Cicogna, Marina. *Ancora spero: Una storia di vita e di cinema*. Venice, 2023.

Damiani, Ludovica. *Set in Cortina: il cinema e le Dolomiti, scatti, protagonisti, racconti*. With an introduction by Paolo Mereghetti. Milan, 2010.

Dolomieu, de Déodat. "Sur un genre de pierres calcaires très peu effervescentes avec les acides et phosphorescentes par la collision," *Journal de physique* (Paris 1791).

Edwards, Amelia B. *Untrodden Peaks and Unfrequented Valleys: A Midsummer Ramble in the Dolomites*. London, 1873.

Gaspari, Francesca, and Maria Luisa Menardi, *Coŝlùpe frìte e lòchi 'n técia: Raccolta di ricette della tradizione ampezzana*. Cortina d'Ampezzo, n.d.

Giacomel, Paolo. *Tar-Kashi 1881: Storia di un'arte indiana a Cortina d'Ampezzo*. Cortina d'Ampezzo, 2008.

Giacomel, Paolo. *La fucina artistica dei "Càiser" dei maestri del ferro battuto Modesto e Ugo Demenego*. Catalogue of the exhibition at the Museo Etnografico delle Regole, Cortina d'Ampezzo, December 22–March 25, 2008. Cortina d'Ampezzo, 2008.

Gilbert, Josiah, and George Cheetham Churchill. *The Dolomite Mountains: Excursions Through Tyrol, Carinthia, Carniola, & Friuli in 1861, 1862, & 1863*. London, 1864.

Grandjean, Maurice. *En Tyrol: Paysages, Mœurs, Histoire, Légendes*. Lille, 1893.

Grießmair, Hans. *Stuben und Möbel im Tiroler Bauernhaus*. Bolzano, 2016.

Hemingway, Ernest. *A Moveable Feast*. New York, 1964.

Magnani, Franco, ed. *I camini di Vietti*. Milan, 1990.

Mancuso, Franco. *Edoardo Gellner: Il mestiere di architetto*. Milan, 1996.

Marzotto, Marta, with Laura Laurenzi. *Smeraldi a colazione*. Milan, 2016.

Montanelli, Indro [under the pseudonym A. Siberia]. "Siamo tutti portogalli." *Il Borghese*, 34 (August 26, 1955).

Montanelli, Indro. *Nella mia lunga e tormentata esistenza: Lettere da una vita*. Milan, 2018.

Niven, David. *The Moon's a Balloon*. London, 1971.

Notte, Lorenzo, ed. *Cortina. Dicono di lei: Le Dolomiti nella letteratura*. Bologna, 2019.

Padovan, Rachele. *La cucina ampezzana: Storia e ricette*. Mulazzo, MS, 2023.

Peria, Vincenzo. *Case di campagna*. Milan, n.d.

Pivano, Fernanda. "A Cortina con Hemingway innamorato." *Corriere della Sera*, December 31, 1997.

Tuckett, Elizabeth. *Zigzagging Amongst Dolomites*. London, 1873.

White, Walter. *On Foot Through Tyrol in the Summer of 1855* (1855). New York, 2016.

Zardini, Stefano. *Cortina*. Cortina d'Ampezzo, n.d.

Zardini Folòin, Stefano, and Nicola Zardini Folòin, eds. *Cortina d'Ampezzo: Ritratto inedito di una signora*. With an introduction by Giovanni Nuvoletti. Cortina d'Ampezzo, 2002.


# BRIEF GLOSSARY OF AMPEZZO

ARFA DELLE FAVE: now almost vanished, this structure made of wooden bars was used to dry fava beans. A tradition of South Tyrolean origin.

BRITE: shepherd's hut.

BRONZIN: rounded bronze vessel with three feet and a movable handle that was placed near the fire for heating water.

BUJE: ventilation holes in barns, usually embellished with religious motifs, crosses and hearts cut into the walls.

FOGHER: the hearth of the old fireplace placed at the center of a room with high benches ranged along two or three sides.

LARIN: Now replaced by the more practical kitchen range, it was an open fire lit on a stone slab set against the walls in a corner and surmounted by a rudimentary hood to expel the fumes.

MALGA: refuge for animals, usually cows.

STUA: living room, with wooden walls, sometimes hinged and decorated ceilings.

TABIÀ: is a construction typical of the valley with a generally sloping floor. The barn and cowshed were once the main elements of the house. They have precise characteristics, including a broad roof that overhangs the outside walls and grows wider at the top. The houses were often built without foundations so that they were almost able to float on the ground and move without forming cracks.

TOULÀ: old rustic barn.

# ACKNOWLEDGMENTS



I would like to thank Mattia Aquila, who accepted this photographic challenge notwithstanding the sometimes extreme conditions of ice, snow, and, above all, a total lack of light.

Marsilio Arte, Emanuela Bassetti, Luca De Michelis, Martina Mian, Carmen Malafronte, Stefano Grandi, Giovanna Ambrosano, and the rest of the team, who had the idea for this book and proposed it to me.

My husband Giovanni for having introduced me to Cortina d'Ampezzo twenty-five years ago.

Franco Sovilla for his wonderful knowledge of Cortina, as well as Elsa Zardini Soriza of the U.L.d'A (Unione de i Ladis de Anpezo), who has taught me so much about Ladin culture.

Once again the Archivio Zeno, with Nicolò and the incomparable Elena Frigerio-Zeno, for having helped me get a feeling for the life of glamourous visitors to the town at the end of the eighteenth century, through their old family photos—along with those of Chiara (Kitt) Donà dalle Rose, Giovanna Cordova, Maria Celeste Marini, Alberto Franchetti, and Lella Di Girolami's marvelous photos of Tito Lebreton.

Thanks also to Emanuele Filiberto of Savoy for researching his personal archives.

My Italian family, Giovanna and Nicola Giol, who were the first to speak to me about Tito Lebreton, and above all Nicola for having preserved his work so well at Ca' dei Fiori, enriching it with his own impeccable style. His sumptuous bird-themed table is a rare testimony to a unique and unrivaled art of living.

All the people, whether I have named them or not, who have not only opened up their homes to me, but have laid truly beautiful tables for us, one finer than the other, in keeping with the themes they were given—pewter, ceramics, game, Christmas... I'm thinking in particular of Carla Alverà, Chantal d'Acquarone, Chiara Reale, Osanna Visconti, Anna Marzotto, and Alessia Bormioli. Thanks, too, to Matteo Marzotto for having re-created down to the smallest details one of his mother Marta's legendary tables.

Much gratitude as well to Marina and Caterina Zangrando, fashionistas mother and daughter both, for having opened up their wardrobes and those of their friends.

And to Michele Schettino and the Valcastello Polo Club for letting us photograph them and their horses.

To my friends in Ampezzo, Stefano and Silvia Gris and Claudio Zanettin, who were the first to introduce me to the local craft culture and the arts of filigree and tarkashi. To Stefano and Silvia Gris in particular for having taken the time to explain the architecture of Edoardo Gellner and Luigi Vietti and for having introduced me to the Santel family.

Congratulations to Gheo Manaigo for having maintained Hemingway's room intact, as well as the marvelous bar of the Hotel de la Poste.

Thanks to the champion skiers Giovanni Dibona and Hubertus and Simona von Hohenlohe for having agreed to pose for us, the latter in their race outfits.

Thanks to the legendary Sci Club 18, for having taught my children to ski and to its active president Amedeo Reale for continuing to inspire new generations.

To Paola Caovilla, the whole of the Zoppas family, and Alessandro Benetton for having shared their memories of the architect Luigi Vietti. To Pupa, Anna, Giovanni and Federica Pellegrini, and Bernardo Rucellai for those of Indro Montanelli and to Silvia Iliceto for having preserved the historic Casa Menardi.

To all those who have bent over backwards to find me the most disparate books on handicrafts and local culture: Maria von Schaffsgotsch, Nicoletta Bombassei, Alexandre Boutry, Catherine Buyse, and Roberto De Feo.

For the gastronomic delights of Cortina, my thanks go to Daniela Alverà of the Pasticceria Lovat, Claudio Alverà of Dolomiti Lodge, Antonio Onorato of Rosa Petra, and Filippo Borghi, the elegant barman of the Hotel de la Poste.

Thanks to Jacques Grange and Pierre Passebon for their French touch in Ampezzo. To Ampezzan Fiori for its flowers, to my friends Bianca Arrivabene, Alessandra Alverà, Idarica Gazzoni, Domitilla Clavarino, Barbara Modulo, the artist Alice Mocellin, Diamara Parodi, Marion Franchetti, Cristina Gnugnoli, Martina Pizzul, and Ginevra Selvatico for their memories and their invaluable aid.

Cortina would not be the same without its skilled artisans, so my thanks go as well to Beppino d'Incà, Matteo Menego, Marco and Renzo Zardini, and to the collectors Luigi Carlon and Giulio Clerici.

Thanks to all friends who have helped me but wish to remain anonymous.

Finally, I must express my gratitude to my French family, who have passed on to me their taste for good books and writing, and to my children Ambra, Leonardo, Amerigo, and Gregorio, who I hope will continue to love and live Cortina d'Ampezzo.

*Cover*
A flowery corner at Valcastello.
The *trompe-l'œil* wall was painted
by Chantal d'Acquarone

*Back cover*
Fabrics in a folk style warm up
corners of the *stube* in Alessia Bianchi
Bormioli's house

*Front endpapers*
Placemat with a retro flavor
by Ricamificio Dolomiti.
Ancient Tyrolean rapresentation
of Winter

*p. 2*
Painted wooden furniture
at Ca' del Rite

*p. 4*
A door richly decorated with folk
motifs at Marta Marzotto's home

*p. 7*
Casa delle Regole, ancient town hall
of Cortina d'Ampezzo

*pp. 8-9, pp. 166-167*
Cortina Cooperative's typical
wrapping papers

*Back endpapers*
Ancient Tyrolean rapresentation
of Summer.
Placemat with a retro flavor
by Ricamificio Dolomiti

*Photo credits*
Archivio GBB / Alamy Foto Stock p. 235
Cinematic / Alamy Foto Stock p. 242
Mondadori Portfolio/Giorgio Lotti p. 236
Moviestore Collection Ltd / Alamy Foto Stock p. 119
Universal Images Group North America LLC / Alamy
Foto Stock p. 126

*Translations*
Huw Evans

*Graphic design and layout*
Carmen Malafronte

*Editing*
Lemuel Caution



*First edition* October 2024
ISBN 979-12-5463-215-4

*Reproduction and printing coordination*
Opero s.r.l., Verona

*Printing*
Grafiche Stella s.r.l., Roverchiara (VR)

*for*
Marsilio Arte® s.r.l., Venice
www.marsilioarte.it

SOMMER

DOL